CONFLICTED:

CONNECTING THE 4 PHASES OF CONFLICT MANAGEMENT THROUGH LOGIC AND EMOTION

MARLENE GONZALEZ

Copyright 2022

All rights reserved. No part of this publication may be reproduced, distributed, or transmitted in any form or by any means, including photocopying, recording, or other electronic or mechanical methods, without the prior written permission of the publishers, except in the case of brief quotations embodied in critical reviews and certain other noncommercial uses permitted by copyright law. For permission requests, contact the author through the website below:

www.marlenegonzalez.com

eBook ISBN: ISBN: 978-1-956253-13-9

Paperback ISBN: 978-1-956253-14-6

Hardcover ISBN: 978-1-956253-15-3 & 978-1-956253-16-0

Audiobook ISBN: 978-1-956253-17-7

CONTENTS

Introduction	13
1. THE NATURE OF CONFLICT	23
Meaning of Conflict	24
Phases of Conflict	26
Characteristics of Conflict	29
Types of Conflict	32
Your Conflict Management DNA	35
The Dangers of Avoiding Conflict	40
Reasons Why You Avoid Conflict	42
Chapter Takeaways	44
2. HISTORY AND CONSEQUENCES OF UNRESOLVED CONFLICT	47
How Your Parents Affected Your Subconscious	48
The High Price of Unresolved Conflict	52
Causes of Office Conflict	55
Learning to Embrace Conflict as a Leader	56
Steps to Embrace Conflict	58
Reaction vs. Response	59
Chapter Takeaways	61
3. STEPPING IN TO RESOLVE CONFLICT	63
Why Conflict is Important	64
Challenging Your Reluctance to Resolve Conflict	69
What is Conflict Resolution?	72
The Ripeness of Conflict	73
Benefits of Resolving Your Conflicts	76
Styles of Conflict Resolution	79

Conflict Resolution Assessment	83
Chapter Takeaways	87

4. HOW YOUR PERSONALITY SHAPES YOUR CONFLICT MANAGEMENT STYLE — 89

What Is Insights Discovery?	90
Understanding the Insights Color Energies	91
How to Work With Color Energies	93
Color Energies and How They Handle Stress	95
Benefits of the Insights Discovery Model	97
Chapter Takeaways	100

5. THE PHASES OF CONFLICT MANAGEMENT — 103

The Four Phases of Managing Conflict	105
Chapter Takeaways	116

6. PHASE I – HOW TO HANDLE DISAGREEMENTS — 119

Learning to Stay Calm	120
The Importance of Active Listening	127
The Steps to Effective Communication	130
Embracing Negative Emotions	137
Resolving Highly Charged Conversations	140
Ground Rules For Handling Disagreements	142
Chapter Takeaways	143

7. PHASE II – CREATING MUTUAL UNDERSTANDING — 147

The Path to Mutual Understanding	148
Facilitating Mutual Understanding Through Empathy	151
How to Develop Empathy	154
Practicing Validation and Empathy	157

	What Does Validation Look Like?	159
	Chapter Takeaways	162
8.	PHASE III – FOCUSING ON SHARED GOALS	165
	Keeping Your Eyes on the Target	166
	How to Build Goodwill	170
	Strengthening the Partnership	172
	How to Preserve the Relationship in a Heated Conflict	174
	What if You Can't Salvage the Relationship?	181
	Chapter Takeaways	182
9.	PHASE IV – THE ROOT OF CONFLICT	185
	Tracing the Origins	186
	Tools For Identifying Potential Causal Factors	190
	Chapter Takeaways	202
10.	PHASE IV – TAKING ACTION	205
	The Path of Negotiation	206
	Rational and Emotional Elements of Negotiation	209
	Distributive vs. Integrative Negotiations	212
	Creating an Optimal Solution	218
	Chapter Takeaways	220
11.	FACILITATING PERSONAL AND PROFESSIONAL CONFLICT RESOLUTION	223
	Resolving Marital Conflicts	224
	How to Resolve a Marital Conflict	227
	Helping Children Handle Conflict	230
	Teaching Children Communication and Problem-Solving Skills	234
	Your Two-Minute Conflict Action Plan	236
	Resolving Workplace Conflicts	236
	Chapter Takeaways	245

12. MAKING YOUR OWN CONFLICT RESOLUTION PLAN	249
Understand the Fundamentals	250
Use Empathy Wisely	251
Pick Your Battles	252
Conflict is About Perspective	253
Conclusion	255
About the Author	265
Also By Marlene Gonzalez	267
References	269

This book is dedicated to creating a peaceful world and the next generation of leaders – on your shoulders lays the responsibility to build a better world.

This book is dedicated to my husband, Carlos – you are my rock and thought partner.

To my publishing team – you are awesome.

JOIN OUR COMMUNITY

Please, don't make this journey alone.

In order to maximize your investment in this book, I encourage you to join our community. As part of our community, you will get valuable content. We often host free book/audiobook giveaways and helpful resources that will be key to your leadership journey.

Wherever people come together, there is the possibility of conflict. This book will give you insights on how to resolve differences anytime, anywhere, and with anyone. Included tools that allow you to understand your style and those of others around you and learn about various tools available so you can customize the ideal solution to any dispute.

To receive the Conflict Management Quiz, Scan the QR code below:

I can't wait to connect with you there,
Your coach, Marlene Gonzalez

"Difficulties are meant to rouse, not discourage. The human spirit is to grow strong by conflict."

— BY WILLIAM ELLERY CHANNING

INTRODUCTION

Today, most people think of conflict as something gone wrong. A relationship that's broken. And there's plenty of examples of conflict gone wrong in the world right now to point to as an example.

But when someone can bring in the different pieces of the broken puzzle and understand how they fit together? They can save their company thousands of dollars in time, expenses, and training, not to mention keep an efficient team in place. At a personal level, it can allow friends and families to stay close and connected - at a time when we need harmony more than ever.

Ready to learn about how the different pieces fit together? Let's dive in!

David is a talented web developer who works for an up-and-coming e-commerce company. He is tasked with designing a new website to enhance user experience and promote the company's services. The goal is to create a website that is catchy, engaging, and user-centric.

This is a huge project for David. Luckily, he has a small team of skilled web developers to back him up. He is also working with a team of debuggers to ensure any errors in the system are identified and removed. This collaboration between developers and debuggers is a critical part of the new website's integration process. After discussing the project with his team leader Samantha, he decides to utilize a relatively new toolkit that provides better results and greater flexibility for future system modifications.

But then a problem occurs.

During the integration process, Frank, one of the debuggers, sends David an important notice about a bug in the system. For some reason, David misses the notice and the website ends up being updated with the bug. As a result, users cannot interact with the website during checkout.

When the error is reported, Frank quickly distances himself from the mistake by blaming David. Frank says he informed David about the bug but never received acknowledgement. As the matter escalates, David is summoned before his team leader as well as the company CEO. He senses a major confrontation on the horizon and knows that Frank's comments regarding his competence have damaged his reputation.

David may be talented, but he's also timid. He's afraid of facing an argument and a potential conflict with his bosses. During the meeting, his breathing is shallow, and his palms are clammy. He's also unable to look anyone in the eye. In such a situation, he feels helpless, unconfident, and in constant dread of any negative remarks about his performance. The fact that Frank is also in the room doesn't make things easier as he maintains David should have been more careful with such an important aspect of the company's operations.

David is afraid of two things. The first is the conflict with his bosses. The second is losing his reputation with his team leader with whom he has a great rapport. The situation seems catastrophic because he has no idea how to respond. He fears Frank will get the upper hand and his opinions will go unheard. Though it's a small mistake easily rectified, David is afraid of leaving a bad impression. As a result, he gets emotional and panicky because he fears conflict. He is even willing to use redundant systems in his work if it would spare him from facing such situations in the future.

Is this scenario familiar to you? Like David, do you also fear and avoid conflict?

One of the clearest signs of conflict is its tendency to trigger stress and put you in a fight-or-flight mode. It is a mental struggle that results from competitive or incompatible needs that are opposed to one another. You could be having a conversation and realize you hold different opinions to the person you're talking with. Conflict is a clash of interests, and without a doubt, you have been part of a conflict at some point in your life.

Maybe you hate the idea of conflict and try to avoid it whenever possible. Say you have a disagreement with your roommate over who should wash the dishes. Instead of confronting the issue and solving the problem, you ignore it. You fear the negative effects of conflict and its impact on your relationship with the other person. You choose to avoid conflict to preserve the friendship.

When a conflict arises, you probably feel trapped and powerless. You don't have the skills to resolve it. Maybe you and your partner argue about spending quality time together. Your emotions are overwhelming, and you cannot see a way out of a confrontation that is quickly escalating. So You use diversionary tactics to sidestep the issue. You change the conversation to avoid talking about it.

Maybe you're the type of person who readily accepts compromises to keep others happy. You'll let things go and not point out your needs, leaving you silently frustrated after a conflict. You convince yourself that you're taking the high road, yet your life is stuck because you're sacrificing your convictions and values. For the sake of "keeping the peace," you never stand up for your opinions or ideas.

It could be that you simply prefer to let conflicts resolve themselves, often without any favorable outcome. You may believe that if you don't actively engage in conflict, it will go away on its own. But the truth is you're afraid to take action when a conflict arises. You often take too long before acting on an issue even as the conflict escalates.

At first glance, it may seem that conflict resolution is a huge mountain that's impossible to climb. It's not! You can conquer conflict if you know the right steps to take. By learning what conflict resolution is and the benefits that come from learning how to resolve different forms of conflict, you can push through this Once you identify your style of conflict management you will know how to handle yourself during a confrontational situation. And as you gain a deeper understanding of conflict resolution, you'll find it easier to hack any conflict.

That's why this book has been so helpful for so many people. I will show you the skills I've learned to resolve both personal and professional conflicts. And as conflicts can occur anywhere, you need to know how to deal with them without fear whether at home or in the office. You will also learn how to navigate tense moments and find useful solutions benefiting both parties. The tips included in this book will help you stay level-headed and stress-free even in a conflict.

Just imagine developing the key skills to handle tough situations as a leader. Creating a better environment that promotes cooperation and resolving conflicts effectively and immediately without damaging productivity.

And even better, you can save relationships not by avoiding conflict but by finding a sense of mutual understanding. You will learn how to focus on shared interests and collaborate harmoniously in the long run.

Conflict is not something you should avoid. When you avoid it, you inhibit your ability to take charge of your life. And avoiding it is based on fear, a negative emotion that makes it much more difficult to achieve your goals, dreams, and responsibilities toward people you care about. We often find ourselves feeling helpless and unable to act when facing conflict. This comes from the fear of what might happen and how the other person may react. It can cause you to recoil and pull away from any situation that may lead to a disagreement.

You might be wondering who I am to know so much about this, and why you should trust my expertise.

Marlene Gonzalez, founder, and president of Life Coaching Group LLC, an organization that focuses on leadership development and executive coaching. I am a renowned executive coach and facilitator and have held many executive corporate positions in the United States, Europe, and Latin America. I'm also the former Senior Director of Global Training, Learning, and Development for McDonald's Corporation.

I know what it's like to deal with conflict at an executive level; I've dealt with it for years!

I also hold a B.S., an Executive MBA/PAG, and a graduate diploma on Managerial Issues in the global enterprise from Thunderbird University. And I'm the author of *Leadership Wizard books*, a coaching series focusing on transformational leadership topics.

I've had the opportunity to coach many people on how to lead their lives. Through this experience, I've discovered most people prefer to avoid direct arguments and let things stay as they are. They choose to skirt the issue even if acting on it would be in their best interests. Their work suffers or their personal life comes to a standstill as they accept life as it is. This is not the kind of life I want for you.

Now don't get me wrong, I've encountered plenty of people who are too aggressive when resolving conflicts. They tend to be pushy and competitive, always seeking to impose their will on others. They prefer to win the argument and get their way at any cost. Unfortunately, they end up destroying the relationship with the other person. This is not the kind of outcome you want, either.

And it can be really hard to find that balance if no one has shown you the skills involved, which is why I ended up writing this book. I want to help you face and manage conflict efficiently. I love to share my experience of studying various psychological techniques and exercises to help you understand what makes a leader confident, assertive and emotionally resilient to stress. I am passionate about sharing my insights on transformational leadership through a combination of Insights Discovery, the psychology of

C.G. Jung, corporate career experience and professional coaching expertise.

Hiding from conflict is not a solution. I want to equip you with the necessary skills, mindset, and tools to help you effectively face and resolve any conflicts you might come across, personally as well as professionally. Conflict is not a bad thing, and it can be resolved without a heated exchange of words. What you need are the right steps to conflict resolution and an understanding of your conflict personality style. This book provides four clear and simple hacks to help you manage personal and professional conflicts.

We are living in a time when conflicts are popping up everywhere you go. I know you've seen it. People are tense and on edge due to all the uncertainty surrounding them. But you cannot be a slave to your fears. By the time you finish reading this book, you should be able to turn any tense situation into a manageable encounter.

I can't wait until you have the confidence to know that no matter the scenario, you can emerge unharmed—even well informed—from conflicts. There's no need to shelter yourself from the fear that conflict triggers in your mind. You will have the tools necessary to guide you along the way. Prepare yourself for a journey that begins with understanding where you stand.

Let's walk this journey together—to discover the nature of conflict and why it's an important aspect of life. Wherever people come together, there is the possibility of conflict.

This book will give you insights on how to resolve differences anytime, anywhere, and with anyone. Included tools that allow you to understand your style and those of others around you and learn about various tools available so you can customize the ideal solution to any dispute. To receive the Conflict Management Quiz, go to: https://marlenegonzalez.com/conflicted or scan the QR code below!

1

THE NATURE OF CONFLICT

You're probably wondering why conflict exists in human society. Wouldn't it be great if we could all just get along? Well, as appealing as that notion may be, the truth is that *conflict will never go away*. Once you begin to understand the nature of conflict, you will realize just how true this statement is.

Society is made up of people with unique personalities and traits. No two people think the same way so there is always going to be a difference in thought processes and levels of understanding. As a result, each individual has their perspective on issues. When two people have different opinions, a conflict is bound to arise. Conflict is really just an argument between two or more people who are unable to find a consensus.

A healthy and functioning society will always have conflicts. We can't avoid this fact. In this chapter, you will learn the significance of conflict in your life and its characteristics and phases. And you'll begin to understand why you're reluctant to deal with conflict as well as the dangers of avoiding it. But first, let's dive into exactly what *conflict* means.

MEANING OF CONFLICT

Picture John and Brian good friends working for a reputable advertising agency. One day, their boss assigns them a major project and asks them to work together as a team. But they have different opinions on how to execute the project and can't resolve their differences. Before you know it, they are at the point where they can't even stand to be in the same room.

This is a classic case of what it means to have a conflict. It arises from a difference in understanding, thought process, interests, attitudes, or perceptions between individuals. It often leads to heated exchanges and can sometimes go as far as physical altercations. If unresolved, a conflict may cause a loss of peace and harmony and damage relationships.

But it isn't just work relationships affected by conflict. It can occur between states, countries, political parties, and even at home. What starts as a minor tiff may end up erupting into a major war if the conflict is not resolved in time. Take, for example, India and Pakistan. Though these two countries have similar cultures, climates and religions, they have been embroiled in a conflict spanning decades. Unresolved issues have now led to a major standoff between two neighboring countries.

Sometimes unresolved issues between countries are taken for granted and allowed to fester because one party believes that it has the upper hand. This kind of attitude in a dispute can lead to bigger problems down the road. Just look at the current global crisis, most conflicts are the result of ego clashes and simple misunderstandings. For example, your friend tells you to meet them at 8 tomorrow at your favorite café. You arrive at the café first thing, but your friend doesn't show up. You call them, but they don't answer. You leave the café in a rage, swearing you're going to give your friend a piece of your mind. You start recalling all the past episodes when they hurt you, yet you said nothing.

When they call you that night, you launch into a scathing attack before they even have a chance to explain their side of the story. This leads to a major fight where a lot of nasty things are said. It's only later on that you both realize the problem. Neither of you specified a clear time to meet. You showed up at 8 a.m., and your friend showed up at 8 p.m.! What started as a minor misunderstanding has led to bruised egos and damaged a friendship.

PHASES OF CONFLICT

So you can see how a conflict begins and grows. Once you understand the evolution of a conflict, you can see how to effectively resolve it. A conflict doesn't just arise out of the blue. There is a pattern every conflict follows.

The pattern usually begins with conflicting needs. So start by learning how to recognize them in your relationships. Be open to exploring conflicting needs with compassion and understanding. Doing so leads to stronger relationships, more cohesive teams, and creative problem-solving.

Once you begin exploring these conflicting needs, you'll realize that a conflict pattern has multiple phases. There are five phases that every conflict goes through.

Prelude phase

The first phase is the prelude to conflict. Conflict arises from differences large and small. It happens when people disagree over core values, principles, motivations, perceptions, ideas or desires. In this phase, all the factors that can potentially create a conflict arise. These factors could be religious, educational, ideological, cultural, etc.

Let's say your teenage son is listening to his favorite punk rock music in his room. It's extremely loud and you can hear it all the way downstairs. All you can think of is how much you hate that music. On top of that, he's supposed to be doing his homework. So you yell at him to turn it down. He turns down the volume, but less than two minutes later, it's back to full blast. You feel a headache coming on and you decide it's time to march upstairs and tell your son exactly what's on your mind.

Triggering event

This phase is when a specific event triggers a conflict. Let's say you barge into your son's room and turn off the music. He starts complaining about you infringing on his personal space. You yell back something about "his" space being inside "your" house. You tell him that he's only allowed to listen to his music at a reasonable volume and only after he's done his homework. He responds by yelling at you to get out of his room.

A conflict such as this may seem trivial. But when it triggers such strong emotions, it's a sign that a deep personal need or fear is at the core of the problem. It might be a need to feel safe and secure, a need to feel respected and valued, or a need for more intimacy. Conflict-triggering fears can range from the fear of confrontation and embarrassment to the fear of losing control of others or outcomes.

Initiation phase

In this phase, there are clear warning signs that a conflict has begun. The rude response by your son now triggers a heated exchange. Voices are raised as you yell at each other about being disrespectful. Old arguments are reopened and hurtful things are said. Your spouse has to intervene to calm things down.

Differentiation phase

This is the phase when the parties involved in the conflict openly express their differences. Your spouse convinces you and your son to sit down at the kitchen table and talk about why you're yelling at each other. You open up about your son constantly refusing to listen or take your advice and how you fear he will soon lose all respect for you. He reveals that he feels his opinion never matters and he's not being allowed to express himself. The conversation goes deeper as more differences in ideas and opinions are laid out.

Resolution phase

This is the most important phase of a conflict and is the primary focus of this book. A conflict cannot be allowed to fester. It may be that past disagreements swept under the rug are contributing to the current conflict. You and your son must come to a compromise that resolves the conflict. If all the underlying issues aren't brought to a conclusion, everyone in the home will suffer. It's time to explore various options to ensure any underlying issues are laid to rest.

CHARACTERISTICS OF CONFLICT

The word "conflict" suggests all kinds of different things for different people. Some imagine war while others may see it like a plague. Some may even feel it is similar to torture or death. The metaphor you use to describe conflict determines how you think and feel about it. If conflict arouses negative images such as war and death, then it's no wonder you avoid it at all costs!

But there is no reason to see conflict in such a negative light. They occur naturally in life. As long as people have diverse needs and seek their own interests, there will always be potential for conflict. Conflicts pop up everywhere, but there are only three major roots. These are:

- **Limited resources** – For example, your partner isn't spending enough time with you.
- **Unmet needs** – For example, your physical, emotional or spiritual needs aren't being met in a relationship, career or your job.
- **Difference in values** – For example, you are engaging with people of different cultures, races, genders, etc.

Let's explore the three roots of conflict, so you can understand the true characteristics of conflict. By recognizing these characteristics, you'll be able to see that conflict comes with potential growth opportunities. The eight characteristics of conflict include:

1. It's a process

Every conflict follows the same process. It begins with a misunderstanding when one party sees another as a threat to their interests. This threat can be due to a difference in values, opinions, ideas or even personal traits. And once the misunderstanding occurs, it often leads to competition, compromise, avoidance, or collaboration.

2. It's inevitable

Let's face it, conflicts occur wherever humans exist. As long as you have two people engaging with one another, some form or level of conflict is inevitable. People are different and though these differences may be minor, there is still the potential for disagreement.

3. It's a normal part of life

In society, people relate to one another at an individual, group, or organizational level. At each level, there are unlimited needs, limited resources, and different values. These discrepancies create a breeding ground for conflict. But conflict doesn't have to be a problem in your life as long as you know how to manage it effectively.

4. It's a perception

A conflict only exists if the individuals interacting with one another see it as such. If you perceive a situation to be a conflict, this will affect your behavior and communication toward the other person.

5. It's based on opposition

A conflict only occurs when you feel something, or someone is opposing your interests. For a conflict to exist, there has to be someone else doing or saying something you don't like.

6. It requires interdependence and interaction

There can be no conflict without a sense of interdependence. Which means there are two people who rely on one another in some way, meaning they are also interacting with each other. And this interaction is what creates the potential for conflict.

7. It affects everyone

Everyone experiences conflict at some point in their life, I'm sure you can think of many examples in your own life. This happens between individuals, within a group, or in organizations.

8. It's multidimensional

A conflict can have many dimensions. It can be caused by a serious issue or a minor one. It can be between total strangers or siblings. It can have the capacity to bring people together or destroy a relationship forever. Look at any conflict you've ever experienced, I bet it had many dimensions to it. By understanding the dimensions involved in your conflict, you stand a better chance of finding a positive outcome.

TYPES OF CONFLICT

So we've seen that conflict can be either constructive or destructive. If you are part of a team, work to ensure whatever conflict arises is constructive and improves the team's performance. If you can identify the type of conflict you're facing, you'll know whether to encourage a dialogue over the issue or stop the debate and move on.

Before you can successfully manage a conflict, you'll need to understand the general ways in which a conflict emerges. Let's start by examining the basis of involvement for the people involved. Conflict may be:

- **Intrapersonal** – Within yourself
- **Interpersonal** – Between people
- **Intragroup** – Between members of one group
- **Intergroup** – Between different groups
- **Intra-organizational** – Within an organization
- **Inter-organizational** – Between different organizations

Next, let's break down conflict into three types. These are task conflict, relationship conflict, and value conflict.

1. Task conflict

This is a disagreement over the results or content of a task. In the workplace, a task conflict may involve the utilization of resources, interpretation of facts or policies or procedures. You'd think this kind of conflict would be easy to resolve, but it often has deeper and more complex roots than you first think. For example, an argument over which team member should present a project at a conference may seem like it's based on who is better qualified. However, the real conflict could be about a sense of rivalry between colleagues.

2. Relationship conflict

This type of conflict is based on interpersonal disagreements within a group. It stems from differences in personality, taste, and communication styles. Let's say you're part of a team involved in a research project. One member is known for belittling teammates' ideas and opinions. When you propose an idea, this person flatly states that your opinion is idiotic and irrelevant. This will trigger a relationship conflict because that member isn't offering a fair assessment of your idea. They just have a personality that is abrasive and rude.

3. Value conflict

This conflict comes from underlying differences in values and identities. These can be religious, political, generational, cultural or ethical values. While some topics are considered taboo in the workplace, a disagreement may arise when a seemingly related policy is implemented. For example, colleagues may disagree over an affirmative action policy. Or a value conflict may arise when your company considers partnering with an organization known to be an environmental polluter.

YOUR CONFLICT MANAGEMENT DNA

Conflict management DNA simply refers to your natural style of dealing with conflicts. So, where do you sit?

On one end are people who tend to avoid conflict like the plague and naturally withdraw from it. On the other end are those who enjoy conflict because they see it as an opportunity to dominate others and have their way. Your conflict management DNA can help you identify your weaknesses and strengths when it comes to how you handle conflict.

But what determines your conflict management style? This is a critical question because it is tied to who you are as an individual. Knowing yourself means having a high level of self-awareness. This makes it easier to know how to handle a conflict in a way that aligns with your ideals. It allows you to resolve conflicts more effectively because you already have an internal roadmap to follow.

Understanding this roadmap can help you make better decisions when faced with conflict. No matter what your conflict management style is, there are four factors that influence how you manage conflict.

1. Past negative experiences

One of the main reasons people are afraid of conflict is past experiences that still haunt them. Let's face it, if you experienced some type of negative outcome from a past conflict, you're going to avoid going through something like that again. It may have happened many years ago in school, at work, or even in a personal relationship. The memory of that experience still leaves a bad taste in your mouth to this day.

Such negative experiences are like triggers that prime you to avoid conflict. Any time you realize you're heading toward a conflict, you experience a wave of emotional turmoil - and you pull away before the conflict occurs.

2. Culture

Cultural differences are the result of having a diverse group of people from different cultures working together. This can pose a major challenge to an organization because each person will see things from their cultural perspective. As a result, you may end up with a group that conflicts in different ways. Some people feel debating or disagreeing with a colleague is disrespectful and don't like it when someone challenges their opinions. Or maybe someone comes from a culture where arguing with raised voices is an acceptable way of engaging with others and thinks nothing of it.

Such differences in culture tend to present the following challenges:

- **Prejudice** – This arises when you have a bias regarding a different race or ethnic group. Though most organizations have diversity training for their employees, sometimes prejudices still slip out via offensive jokes or behavior.
- **Cultural gaps** – Every culture has its social perspective and communication style. In America, with its incredibly diverse cultural mix, workplace communication can be a problem. This is especially true when an employee's culture doesn't mix well with that of the company.
- **Language barriers** – Diversity in culture often means diversity in language. Someone who isn't a native English speaker may struggle to converse effectively with a colleague whose first language is English. You have to be careful when speaking, especially when using slang someone else might not understand.
- **Religious differences** – When you don't

understand someone's belief system, you may be biased against them. Religious differences are touchy subjects that should be avoided as they can easily create conflict in the workplace.
- **Gender discrimination** – In some cultures, sexism is a common occurrence. Someone from a patriarchal culture may inadvertently say or do something that shows gender discrimination. They may find themselves offending others without even knowing it.

3. Generational differences

Today's workplace includes employees from three different generations. This generational gap can create friction as the collective personalities of each group clash with another. And when you add the large gap between their political interests, communication styles, work ethic, attitude toward authority, and technological use? Phew, things can get tough. These three generations are:

Baby Boomers

These are people born between 1946 and 1964. They tend to work long hours, prefer open communication and collaboration, and value face-to-face meetings. They respect authority and expect colleagues to show similar dedication. Statistics show that American Baby

Boomers are more than 70% white. They tend to perceive immigrants as a threat to their traditional values, creating a point of conflict with more racially diverse generations.

Generation X

These are people born between 1965 and 1982. They tend to be very independent and prefer a healthy work-life balance. This means they may not enjoy an authoritarian manager or work long hours like Baby Boomers do.

Millennials

They were born between 1983 and 2004. Millennials prefer to be coached and mentored at work—a far cry from the independent Gen X'ers. They also prefer communicating via technology and hate being forced to read lengthy printed memos. The other generations perceive Millennials to be pampered and idealistic with a poor work-life balance due to excessive use of social media.

4. Risk-aversion

It is said that our strongest instinct is the need to keep things familiar. In other words, most people tend to avoid risk at all costs. This can be a big problem if you stick with the familiar even though it no longer serves your best interests. Sometimes we don't even realize we are staying in an uncomfortable situation simply because it's what we've always done in the past.

Running from risk can cripple your life in many ways. Anything worth doing in life carries some risk, whether it's entering a relationship, asking for a job, or sitting an exam. Without risk, you cannot reach your full potential. Risk aversion is one of the reasons why people avoid conflict. In a conflict, you never know where the disagreement may lead, and many people find this lack of certainty stressful.

THE DANGERS OF AVOIDING CONFLICT

You may think avoiding conflict is a good way to deal with an uncomfortable issue. The truth is that doing so can keep you trapped in it. Avoiding conflict doesn't eliminate the tension. It does quite the opposite.

Picture the scene:

Your boss asks you to discipline a member of your team. Although you're the leader, you hate confrontation, so you do everything to escape the situation. You start finding excuses to leave the office whenever your team member is around. Has that solved the issue? No, it hasn't. The colleague you were supposed to reprimand continues with their behavior because you are avoiding conflict.

And there are other ways people avoid conflict. Sometimes it comes in the form of sugar-coating issues, justifying bad behavior, or acting aggressively to squash any discussion about a contentious issue. None of these actions resolves the problem. For example, colleagues may tolerate each other's behavior even when it's ruining their work relationship. Instead of talking it out, they justify the behavior or assume the problem will go away on its own. And so, the underlying issue grows, resentment increases and those involved become more distant. Before you know it, they are powerless to resolve the situation.

An organization where people avoid conflict doesn't function well for long. Employees with good ideas don't speak up and people end up creating silos. The information doesn't flow freely as it should and difficult issues are swept under the rug. This can lead to business failure because things may be going wrong but no one is bold enough to say something to the leaders. By avoiding conflict, you may end up making things worse not just for yourself but for others as well.

REASONS WHY YOU AVOID CONFLICT

Approach a random person on the street and ask them how they deal with conflict. Most will tell you they generally try to avoid it. Since most people describe conflict using negative metaphors, it makes sense they would try to stay away from it. Yet the same people will tell you conflict avoidance isn't an effective strategy. But if the strategy doesn't work, why is conflict avoidance so common?

Many people avoid conflict because it evokes negative emotions. As you know, confronting and disagreeing with someone involves a lot of tension and uncertainty. The usual stress responses are activated and you're likely to lose control of yourself. Displaying emotions in this way can leave you feeling vulnerable, and nobody likes feeling that way in public. The best way to control yourself during a conflict is to understand why you respond the way you do.

First, let's look at the major reasons why people avoid conflict. Then you can figure out how to overcome your own negative perception of conflict and change your approach accordingly. Here are four reasons that explain why you may avoid conflict:

1. You lack confidence

This is probably the biggest reason why you–and most people–shy away from conflict. You don't feel confident raising an issue because you think the things won't end peacefully. You don't feel confident that you can control the situation. You assume there will be an argument instead of a conversation and that you're likely to lose the disagreement.

2. You perceive determination as rigidity

Sometimes you may want to propose an idea, but you get the sense the other person is too set on following a different path. You keep quiet and go along with their idea to avoid conflict. But what you see as rigidity or dominance may simply be the other person's determination. Just because someone is enthusiastic about something doesn't mean they aren't willing to accept other suggestions.

3. Your family was conflict-avoidant

If you come from a background where people never expressed difficult emotions or you were punished for speaking out, you're likely to avoid conflict. Interaction with your family during childhood creates a model that impacts how you express your needs. It also affects how you treat others during tense conversations.

4. You're stressed out

Whenever you feel stressed out, you automatically have a lower tolerance for more stress in your life. You may be unable to mentally or emotionally cope with any kind of conflict.

Now that you understand the nature of conflict, you're probably wondering whether it's better to seek out conflict or keep avoiding it. The truth is, there is no straight answer. Understanding your personality affects the way you deal with conflicts is key. Hopefully, this chapter has shown you that conflict resolution can lead to growth. It can take you down a path of self-discovery where you ultimately find out which conflict management style best fits your personality.

CHAPTER TAKEAWAYS

Culture is a factor in every conflict. It may not cause the conflict but it always influences it. Whether within a family, community, or organization, culture is part of every conflict that arises. For example, the conflict between a parent and child is influenced by generational culture. A conflict between husband and wife is shaped by gender culture. The conflict between Israel and Palestine may seem territorial, yet it is influenced by identity culture. This is why we need to understand the connection between culture and conflict. Here are some points to consider about culture:

- It is multilayered. Instead of making cultural generalizations about someone, spend time building a relationship and getting to know them more deeply.
- It is always changing. When conditions change, the culture adapts.
- Don't assume that a group has a static culture. Remember to account for context, time, and individual differences.
- It is elastic. Just because you know a person's cultural norms, it doesn't mean the person conforms to them. Treat them as an individual rather than a member of a group.
- It exists below the surface. Take time to study the stories, rituals, and metaphors a person uses to understand their deeper cultural dimensions.
- It can become a narrow identity when threatened or misunderstood. When you feel an aspect of your cultural identity is threatened, you forget all the other aspects that define your identity. It becomes an all-or-nothing battle. This fixation on a narrow identity leads to intractable conflicts.

In the next few chapters, we'll talk about conflict management styles and how your personality influences your preference for or against conflict. When you become more self-aware and begin to understand your personality, you'll realize it's easier to change and improve how you manage conflicts. Knowing yourself well sets the foundation for opening yourself up to better connect with others. So, let's learn about some of the consequences of unresolved conflicts.

2

HISTORY AND CONSEQUENCES OF UNRESOLVED CONFLICT

There is no denying that many of the events you experienced in your past are influencing your attitude today. It can be something that happened decades ago during your childhood or an event you were involved in last week. You have all these emotions from your past affecting your current state of mind, but you're probably not aware of them.

Though you may think the past events are no longer relevant, the truth is they affect your current attitude toward life. Your attitude isn't fixed. It is always changing. The more you interact with others in social situations, the more you expose yourself to experiences that influence who you are today and in the future. This happens due to neuroplasticity, which is your brain's capacity to continually change based on your environment, emotions, thoughts, and behavior.

These factors all end up affecting your conflict management DNA. In the previous chapter, we talked about how certain events can trigger an emotional response that leaves you scared of or troubled by conflict. These unconscious emotions are linked to unresolved trauma you mostly experienced during childhood.

Now, let's explore how your childhood influences your subconscious and affects you today as an adult. We'll consider what happens when conflicts are left unresolved for too long and why leaders should always be prepared to handle conflict.

HOW YOUR PARENTS AFFECTED YOUR SUBCONSCIOUS

The average parent doesn't usually consider their child's subconscious. As a parent, your primary concerns are your child's nutrition, education, health, safety, socialization, and maybe sleep patterns. You invest a lot of time in some things, but you may rarely think about how your child's mind works.

This is because adults tend to view children as little grown-ups. As a result, many parents assume a child should reason and behave like an adult. This is why a parent will try to correct a child's behavior through punishment. They may sometimes use words and actions that traumatize the child. They believe the child should know better—as if the child's mind works the same way as an adult one. But it doesn't. To understand how a child's mind works, you need to understand human brainwaves.

There are five types of brainwaves. These are:

- **Gamma waves** – These are generated when you are engaged in high-level cognitive functions such as solving a tough math problem.
- **Beta waves** – These are generated when you're simply awake.
- **Alpha wave**s – These are generated when you are transitioning from wakefulness to sleep.
- **Theta waves** – These are generated when you are asleep or daydreaming.
- **Delta waves** – These are the slowest brain waves in humans. They are mostly seen in infants.

An adult who is awake is usually in a beta state. However, children don't experience alpha waves until age 6 and beta waves until age 12. In other words, any child under 6 is most likely in theta or delta state even when awake. Children's brainwave frequencies are simply slower than those of adults.

On top of that, the right side of a child's brain develops before the left side. The right brain is responsible for imagination, intuition, and creativity while the left-brain controls logic and reason. This means a child cannot reason like an adult. Up until age 8, a child relies on their parents to identify and process their experiences. It is during this time that a child learns to identify and associate an event as positive or negative. These associations create a life script for the child that will be followed into adulthood.

Keep in mind the child still doesn't know right from wrong because they haven't developed logic or reasoning. Yet they are already accumulating a series of identifications and associations that trigger their emotions. For example, when a child sees a dog barking at them, they sense danger and experience fear. Thus, they associate any dog with a feeling of fear.

It is at this period of development when a child's subconscious programming occurs. Children under age 8 don't have a filter to protect their subconscious. They are experiencing theta brainwaves and going through life in a dream state. They will take everything a parent says literally, including hurtful words and limiting beliefs. Everything they experience with their senses is perceived to be a fact. Like sponges, children absorb the words and emotions of their parents. This ends up shaping their attitude toward life.

If your father was sometimes loud or harsh when you talked to him, you may grow up believing that a conversation always leads to angry outbursts. If your mother constantly yelled at you, you may feel rejected and timid. If your parents rarely paid attention to you, you may grow up feeling insignificant and unable to speak up for yourself. Maybe you were bullied on the school playground and nobody was there to defend you.

As an adult, you now find yourself still dealing with these same issues but in a different form. You may be risk-averse, shy or a people-pleaser. You avoid conflict because you were programmed from a young age to identify and associate any serious engagement with negative emotions. If your boss is displeased with your work and calls for a one-on-one meeting, you may feel afraid because you believe they will shout and write you up. You agree with your colleagues even when you have better ideas because you'd rather keep them happy than engage in a tough conversation. The fear and pain from childhood are stuck in your subconscious mind and control you to this day. Unfortunately, there is a price to pay for not dealing with unresolved conflicts.

THE HIGH PRICE OF UNRESOLVED CONFLICT

These unresolved issues can compromise your ability to lead and be effective in your everyday choices. You may become so fearful of these emotional triggers that you start to avoid addressing any issues that build up within or around you. And then you end up with a string of unresolved conflicts. If you're the leader of an organization, these unresolved conflicts can negatively impact your leadership value, your team, and the whole organization.

It's not easy to see the negative impact of unresolved conflict as it occurs. It usually takes some time before you realize things are going wrong. For example, you may only wake up to the problem when there are a series of missed deadlines, low morale, or more resignations.

But there's no need to wait until things start going wrong to take action. There are specific signs that indicate unresolved conflicts in the workplace. By learning these indicators, you can avoid any resulting long-term damage. Unresolved conflict can be categorized into three groups depending on the level of impact:

1. First-order impacts

These include:

- Poor quality work
- Communication failures
- Rumors
- Missed deadlines
- Leadership distractions (e.g., dealing with complaints)

2. Second-order impacts

These include:

- Split into factions
- Low morale
- Employee turnover
- Less collaboration/trust
- Increase in management scrutiny

3. Third-order impacts

These include:

- Dissatisfied customers
- Loss of employee confidence in management
- Loss of support from upper management
- Inability to retain or recruit talent

- A toxic work culture

If you're working with others, then yes, conflict is inevitable. Instead of running from it, try to focus on its constructive aspects. Most people perceive conflict to be negative because they have experienced more negative than positive aspects.

But how do you know when an ongoing conflict is destructive or constructive?

Here are some of the signs of a destructive conflict:

- The group becomes polarized and divided.
- There is no change in behavior and the problem stays unresolved.
- The individuals or team lose morale.
- Energy is diverted away from priorities.

Here are the signs of a constructive conflict:

- The problem is resolved.
- Bottled-up emotions are acknowledged and released safely.
- There's an open discussion where the underlying issues are laid bare.
- Diverse solutions are explored.

- The parties involved learn and grow from the conflict.

Most managers struggle to handle conflict effectively because they haven't been coached on how to identify its common triggers. They haven't been trained on how to spot their own vulnerabilities when it comes to conflict. And so they are unable to choose solutions that generate constructive outcomes.

CAUSES OF OFFICE CONFLICT

Several factors can trigger conflict in the workplace. Some are due to the *organization's systems*. These include organizational structures, unclear roles, competition, unrealistic deadlines, and inadequate staffing. Others are due to *interpersonal relationships*. These include personal prejudice, cultural differences, differences in priorities, false assumptions, and personality differences.

In many organizations, the most difficult conflicts to manage are those created by a combination of these two factors. By learning how to differentiate the roots of the conflict's causes, you can proactively handle and constructively resolve conflicts, especially if you are in a leadership position.

Poor conflict management is one of the biggest elements that can derail your career as a business leader. By learning how to resolve conflicts effectively, you can reduce corporate costs and ensure organizational stability. I strongly believe that every leader at every level should learn the tools necessary to proactively facilitate constructive conflict resolution.

LEARNING TO EMBRACE CONFLICT AS A LEADER

Michael is a talented and qualified advertising agent. He works hard, has years of experience, and is popular among his colleagues. He is always eager to share his ideas and help out anyone who needs it. But Michael has a problem.

Steve, his boss, doesn't see him in such a positive light. Steve sees him as a know-it-all who challenges and critiques his ideas. And while Steve knows Michael doesn't show these traits in front of others, Steve suspects Michael wants to take over his job. Steve decides to deal with the threat decisively and it's not long before Michael is forced to leave the company.

This is how some leaders choose to deal with conflict. They cannot handle it constructively, so they resort to destructive means. Instead of talking to Michael, Steve avoided conflict by getting rid of him. Steve hasn't yet learned how to properly handle conflict.

The consequences of taking such action against an employee may be bigger than you expect. It could be an indication of a more systemic problem in the organization. This means other employees may also bear the brunt of a leader who hasn't learned how to embrace conflict.

It can lead to lost time, harassment, low productivity, grievances, and reports being filed with employee tribunals. These outcomes can cost the company money and time. On top of that, stifling conflict in an organization can destroy creativity and expertise. As a leader, avoiding conflict can deprive you of useful information from your frontline workers. Employees may be afraid to speak up even when things are going wrong. Ultimately, there will be no flow of ideas to improve the business or workplace relationships.

As you can see, avoiding or stifling conflict can have damaging consequences. If conflict is inevitable, the best thing to do is to handle it in a way that benefits everyone involved. One of the benefits is that it strengthens the harmony of the team. If handled well, a conflict can create an opportunity to explore a new perspective. This can lead to further innovation and development of products and services.

Conflict can also be a tool to share ideas in a way where everyone gets the chance to speak up. This way, conflict becomes more of a fruitful discussion than a shouting match. Constructive conflict also creates an avenue for progress, learning, and growth of individuals as well as the team.

Another benefit is that conflict enables you to know more about your colleagues' personalities. This can improve relationships within the organization and subsequently enhance job satisfaction and retention rates.

STEPS TO EMBRACE CONFLICT

By now you have a better understanding of how conflict can be beneficial if managed properly. But what can you do to embrace constructive conflict? The first step is to reframe your perspective on what conflict means. Conflict doesn't need to have a negative connotation. Try shifting your mindset and see it as beneficial. If you see conflict as an opportunity, you will welcome and encourage it as such.

Secondly, you should question your organization's culture and ethos. Is the culture open to constructive criticism or are people victimized for pointing out problems? Is creativity promoted or do leaders simply look for people to blame for failures? Create a culture where employees are allowed to take appropriate risks and even make mistakes. View this as a way of continuous improvement and growth. Keep in mind that changing an organization's culture must be led from the top. It won't work if senior management asks mid-level and frontline employees to make changes, but they don't do the same.

Thirdly, create a psychologically safe space within your organization where employees can meet and brainstorm ideas that challenge the status quo. Allow your team to engage in sessions where they critique old practices and come up with new ones. If there is a problematic issue affecting the team or a mistake has been made, encourage everyone to focus on solutions. Emphasis should be on improvement going forward and not on attacking the individual who made the mistake.

REACTION VS. RESPONSE

Changing your mindset and reframing your perspective on conflict begins with a decision. It has to be a conscious and deliberate choice and not something you leave to chance. If your decision-making is on autopilot, you'll end up being unconsciously controlled by your emotions. You'll find yourself saying things in anger or frustration during a disagreement. Before you know it, the conflict is out of control and difficult to manage.

Instead of reacting emotionally, learn to respond. Take a few seconds to breathe and think so you don't blurt out the first thought that comes to mind. If someone says something that makes you angry, take a brief pause to ask yourself some questions. "Why did he say that?", "Is it something I said or did?" Your inner curiosity may shed some light on where the other person is coming from.

And don't forget to listen to what the other person is saying. Engage them in conversation so you can understand their perspective. Most people act like they're listening, but they aren't. They are just waiting for an opportunity to interrupt. Learn to actively listen instead of waiting to jump in with your views.

Concentrate on using softer words or phrases that sound less offensive. For example, instead of telling someone to "stop" speaking, ask them to "pause." Avoid the temptation to tell someone, "I understand" as they are likely to react angrily with, "No, you don't understand." A better phrase would be "That must be hard for you." You should also use phrases like "Thank you for sharing your opinion,", "I partially agree with your point of view but here is where we differ," or "It is important for me to …" Or perhaps "Would you agree to see my point of view and explore solutions that will benefit us both?"

When challenging someone's opinion, limit your use of "Why?" Asking this question too often during a tense conversation may come across as hostile. Finally, sprinkle your conversation with positive words like "Yes", "Please" and "Thank you." You've got nothing to lose by being kind and positive.

CHAPTER TAKEAWAYS

As a leader, you should know how to facilitate conflict in a constructive way. Your ability to shepherd constructive conflict determines whether you can create an innovative team that performs at a high level. Here are some questions to help you gauge your skills in supporting constructive conflict:

- *Do I take the time to listen and make others feel heard?*
- *Am I open to alternative points of view?*
- *Do I make my intentions clear when giving criticism to my team?*
- *Do I shy away from giving my opinions?*
- *Do I help my team members clarify their concerns?*

- *Do I encourage others to try new things and experiment?*
- *Am I proficient at reading and responding to nonverbal messages?*

Some of these suggestions in this chapter may sound basic but you would be surprised by the number of times people fail to use them when dealing with conflict. If you discover that either you or your organization doesn't have the right mindset or skill set to handle conflict constructively, it's time to learn how.

Next, let's learn about some of the different styles of conflict resolution and how they can benefit you.

3

STEPPING IN TO RESOLVE CONFLICT

So far we've talked about why most people are naturally inclined to avoid conflict and are often reluctant to step in and resolve it. This may be due to past negative experiences, risk aversion, lack of confidence, or cultural and generational differences. But choosing to avoid conflict by pretending it doesn't exist isn't an effective strategy in the long term. Conflicts are inevitable and if left unresolved can have serious impacts on individuals as well as an organization.

As a leader, part of your responsibility is to guide those under you. Conflicts can disrupt relationships and prevent meaningful work from getting done. By changing your mindset and learning conflict management skills, you will be better equipped to step in and resolve conflicts around you. You'll also be able to teach others how to resolve a conflict in a constructive way.

But what can you do to resolve conflicts? In this chapter, you will learn how to challenge your tendency to avoid conflict. You'll go deeper into what conflict resolution is and when you should step in as a leader. We'll also cover the five styles of conflict resolution and how you can identify the one most suitable for you. But first, let's look at some of the benefits of conflict.

WHY CONFLICT IS IMPORTANT

In Chapter One, we discussed the characteristics of conflict. We talked about why conflict is inevitable and a normal part of life. Whenever you have individuals living or working together, there is going to be some level of conflict. This is especially true in the workplace. With so many employees with different personalities and values working together, there is bound to be conflict. As a leader, it's your job to ensure these conflicts are managed properly so they don't interfere with the organization's objectives. But how do you do this?

As a leader, you should create an environment where your team views conflict positively. This is only possible if your team understands the positive aspects of conflict. You should create a psychologically safe space where your team can openly speak their mind, take risks, and have disagreements without fear of repercussions. This will encourage your team to embrace disagreements and confrontations in a healthy way.

The more your team embraces conflict, the more they will see its many benefits at the individual and organizational level. They will understand why conflict is important and how it can enhance teamwork and productivity. Below are 10 reasons why conflict is important:

1. Generates new ideas

Conflict is a useful tool to fine-tune ideas, generate new solutions and develop trust with others. By engaging someone in a peaceful disagreement, you can refine and uncover flaws in your perspective. Hearing someone else's opinion can clarify your ideas and help make them better. And are you ready for this? A conflict may reveal the opposing ideas aren't as good as your own. This can make you more committed to your original perspective.

2. Opportunities to speak your truth

Sometimes you fail to get what you want because you haven't verbalized your needs. Maybe you lack the assertiveness to clearly state what you want, which lets others impose their needs on you. Conflict may be the best opportunity to speak up for yourself and let others know where you stand. This will make you more resilient and courageous when asking for something in the future.

3. Makes you more flexible

Conflict involves a back-and-forth dialogue between people. This means everyone involved can learn something new and potentially adjust their opinion. Let's face it, you can't be right all the time or win every argument. Conflict teaches you to be open and humble toward others. Both are traits that define a good leader.

4. Improves your listening skills

The goal of conflict and confrontation shouldn't be to win the argument and rub the other person's face in it. It should be to listen to that person's perspective and come to an agreement that works for you both. People who don't listen well tend to become domineering and defensive. By learning how to actively listen, you increase your ability to gain information and make smart decisions.

5. Improves relationships

People who have a good relationship know how to read and decode each other's behavior patterns. Through conflict, you can learn how others think, work, and communicate, especially when under pressure. This provides a certain level of predictability that enables you to work harmoniously with others. You get to know and respect people's limits and interact with them without being offensive.

6. Creates innovation

Most organizations don't embrace change even when it's needed. Yet regular innovation and development are necessary to adapt to market changes and consumer behavior. If the business is to grow, people within the organization must be willing to challenge the status quo and engage in disagreements. And that means conflict can motivate and inspire innovation and invention.

7. Improves your communication skills

Conflict can help you improve your communication skills. A good communicator needs patience, self-control, and intelligence. These are all traits you can develop by engaging in regular conflict. This doesn't mean you should create or look for disagreements. It simply means you shouldn't be afraid to take part in a conflict when it arises.

8. Helps you set boundaries

If you don't set boundaries for other people, they'll assume you don't have any. Conflict provides the perfect opportunity to let others know where you stand and what your limits are. You can communicate your boundaries so others can be respectful of you and your work.

9. You learn emotional control

Emotional control means staying calm under pressure, being direct with your speech, and remaining flexible when engaging with others. Conflict allows you to practice these characteristics so you can improve over time. Most people assume conflict is all about displaying emotions. Flip that around and use it as a tool for gaining more emotional control.

10. Let's you differentiate yourself

You are not like other people. You are different in how you see the world around you, which means you have your own truth. Differentiation is the ability to stand in your truth even as you interact with others who don't share your perspective. Conflict provides you with an opportunity to let others know who you are and what you believe in. Speaking your truth is also good for your health and relationships.

CHALLENGING YOUR RELUCTANCE TO RESOLVE CONFLICT

Avoiding conflict may seem like a good way of not dealing with tense emotions. After all, who wants to deal with the anger, fear, and the anxiety of not knowing what the other person might say or do during a disagreement? However, the longer you wait to address a conflict, the more damage it does to the relationship. This can create a rift between you. When valuable opinions are not openly expressed or shared, it gives way to doubt and mistrust.

As a leader, you can decide to be proactive and work effectively through the conflict. This can strengthen relationships and encourage both parties to find amicable and creative solutions. But how do you go about challenging your reluctance to manage conflicts? Here are a few tips to help you get started.

The first is to make a conscious decision to start seeing conflicts as problems to be solved. This creates a sense of urgency that forces you to act quickly and decisively before the problem gets worse. If you want to avoid conflicts, try to address disagreements as early as possible. This way, you can prevent any escalation that may lead to a full-blown conflict.

Secondly, look within and ask yourself some questions. "What am I concerned about?", "What is preventing me from dealing with this conflict directly?","Why am I afraid?" Such questions can help you really think about your underlying reasons for avoiding conflict. You'll realize that deep down is a fear that is probably holding you back. As Franklin D. Roosevelt said, "The only thing we have to fear is fear itself." This applies to conflicts as well. Once you identify your underlying fears about conflict, you can learn how to overcome these limitations. After identifying your fears, try to figure out what you can do to prevent them from being realized. It can be as simple as taking some time to defuse simmering tensions between colleagues or team members. Get people together—even if it's in an informal setting—and let them talk it out. This can ensure that conflict does not materialize later on.

Think about the consequences of not resolving the conflict. If you find yourself reluctant to deal with it, you should seriously contemplate what the outcome of that unresolved conflict might be. This thought exercise can help you stay motivated when acting to resolve a conflict. It is the best way to identify and assess conflicts that may become serious if not handled quickly.

Also, search out people who know how to handle conflict. You've probably watched someone who deals with conflict really well. It could be a friend, family member, or colleague. Sit down with them and ask how they assess a conflict situation. Ask how they motivate themselves to address issues in a conflict. Ask how they keep the discussion focused on a win-win solution. You'll learn more about this later in the chapter when we'll be discussing styles of conflict resolution.

And as you ask others for their advice, don't forget to request feedback about your approach to conflict. Ask them for suggestions on what you could do differently. If you're locked into an approach that isn't working, asking for feedback can help you break out of detrimental behaviors. It's also possible you've been making progress with your approach without realizing it. Getting external feedback may help you see just how far you've come.

Finally, once you're confident and ready to tackle conflicts, it's time to implement conflict resolution strategies.

WHAT IS CONFLICT RESOLUTION?

Conflict resolution is a mechanism that allows two or more people to settle a disagreement peacefully. Whenever a disagreement arises, the best thing to do is negotiate a peaceful solution as quickly as possible, to prevent the conflict from getting worse. And if possible, talk about it in a way that improves the relationship between the people involved.

But are there specific reasons why you should resolve conflict?

As mentioned before, the primary goal of conflict resolution is to reach a peaceful agreement that benefits all involved. But there are three other reasons why conflict resolution is important:

- It allows you to connect more with people who have different backgrounds, beliefs, or ideas. Resolving a conflict encourages you to examine the other side's perspective and motivations.
- It encourages relationship growth. Resolving a conflict can increase your allies and guide collaboration.
- It prevents you from wasting valuable resources on full-blown battles. By finding a peaceful

solution, you can save energy, time, money, and reputation.

As you can see, conflict resolution plays a critical role, especially in the workplace. But is there a good time to resolve a conflict? Or should you step in at the first hint of a disagreement?

THE RIPENESS OF CONFLICT

There are times when conflict among employees doesn't need a manager's intervention. Sometimes they just need time and space to argue their case and come to an amicable conclusion themselves. This can enhance the working relationship within a team and boost innovation and productivity. But sometimes a conflict may be so detrimental to work performance that it needs immediate intervention.

A leader should know when it's the right time to intervene and resolve a conflict at work. For example, two employees may continue fighting over an issue because each is refusing to cede ground to the other. As the leader, you may realize the fight is affecting their performance and decide it's time to step in. Getting the timing wrong could make the difference between sorting out the issue and damaging the relationship.

Knowing when a conflict is ripe for resolution is an important skill. Learning when to step in will be useful regardless of the type of conflict. Here are some of the warning signs that can let you know when it's time to step in and seek immediate resolution to a conflict:

Sudden changes in behavior

If you notice an employee's behavior has radically changed due to a conflict, it's time to intervene and help the parties reach an amicable solution. Watch out for a sudden change in tone or body language in either party involved in the conflict.

Increased absence from work

As a leader in the organization, you may notice the employees involved in the conflict are taking more sick days than normal. These increased absences are a clear sign that the conflict has reached a critical point.

Increase in stress levels

The parties involved may begin to experience increased stress, anxiety, anger, and hopelessness. This is a sign they lack the mental resources to sustain the conflict because it's been going on too long.

Escalating costs

Once you get embroiled in a legal dispute, you know those lawyer fees will drain your pocket. Drawn-out court cases can be very expensive so you should try to settle the dispute before any costs incurred become overwhelming. The costs may be emotional rather than financial. At some point, you may realize that both parties are mentally and emotionally drained from the fighting. This may be a sign to resolve the issue without allowing it to do any more damage.

Loss of productivity

It's hard to sustain a high level of productivity when you're under mental and emotional stress from a conflict. This can get worse if you're also incurring financial losses as well. Reduced productivity is not good for an organization and is an indication the conflict is ripe for resolution.

There's a time to sit back and let employees deal with their issues. But as a leader, you have a responsibility to keep an eye on the situation and intervene when you see the signs we've talked about. At the end of the day, your goal should be to devise a strong and durable conflict resolution system that deals with problems at the right time and leaves all parties satisfied.

BENEFITS OF RESOLVING YOUR CONFLICTS

We've talked about the fact that the modern workplace involves varying levels of institutional and interpersonal conflict. A lot of time and energy is spent on preventing or managing conflict, so it doesn't create too much disharmony among employees. And we've covered the reality that conflict is an important component of any relationship. Now you know conflict is neither inherently bad nor good and it all comes down to how you perceive the situation.

Apart from perception, there is an influencing element to consider. Although conflict may be beneficial, the most important factor is the way it is handled. Understanding how to resolve conflict effectively when it arises is the key to unlocking the benefits of conflict. By understanding the benefits of resolving conflicts, you can then fully engage in resolution.

Effective mechanisms are necessary to resolve disagreements both personal and professional. Later, we'll talk about the conflict management process and how you can use it to properly engage with conflict. For now, let's explore six benefits of conflict resolution.

1. It lowers costs

Effective conflict resolution increases employee engagement and idea-sharing. This means your team can make better decisions in the workplace. New projects can be implemented effectively because the team is more cohesive and has learned to settle disputes amicably. With better decisions and improved team unity, the organization can improve its bottom line and generate a greater return on its investment.

2. Builds relationships

An unresolved conflict usually gets worse or, at the very least, things stay the same. But through conflict resolution, constructive changes take place and people work through the problem together. Though the process may not be easy, struggling together to resolve the issue ultimately strengthens relationships.

3. Enhances commitment

By taking the step toward resolution, both parties are showing their commitment to the process. It unites those involved and encourages them to face the challenge together as a team. They no longer see the disagreement as a contest between "us" and "them."

4. Enhances productivity

Effective conflict resolution boosts workplace cohesion. This reduces absenteeism while promoting teamwork and creative innovation. Employees also learn how to stay calm under pressure and make better decisions in their work. And so the organization experiences more productivity and efficiency.

5. Higher employee retention

A functional conflict resolution mechanism improves the relationship between employees and management. It provides an avenue to resolve grievances, keep communication channels open and engage team members. And we all know that a stable and functional work environment translates to less employee turnover.

6. Risk management

If left unchecked, conflicts can spiral into aggression, sabotage, and violence. This isn't just bad for relationships, but it could pose a legal risk for an organization. By resolving conflicts effectively, you protect your organization's public perception and brand.

STYLES OF CONFLICT RESOLUTION

Conflicts are inevitable when working in groups, so every leader must learn to manage them. Conflict management involves resolving disputes in a way that minimizes negative results and prioritizes positive ones. It is a critical management skill that requires diverse strategies depending on the situation. Though there are different approaches, some are simply more effective than others.

But understanding which approach to apply depends on the parties involved as well as the situation, you have a real chance at resolving the disagreement. Each conflict management style has its pros and cons, so you'll need to assess the situation and then choose an appropriate style. Understanding different conflict management styles is key because no one solution works in all situations.

By studying various conflict management styles, you will have the guidelines necessary to help you resolve all kinds of conflict. You will know which style to use and even when to switch from one to another. Here are the five styles of conflict management:

1. Avoiding

This is sidestepping or/and ignoring the situation altogether. One or both people may decide the conflict isn't worth engaging in and simply let it fizzle out. This style is used when the conflict is meaningless or there's no time to spend on it. As a manager, you may decide to reassign the conflicting parties to different projects or departments.

This gives them time to cool down as well as some space to adjust their perspectives. However, you should be careful not to push back conflicts indefinitely as they may resurface and explode down the line. Overusing this style risks you coming across as incompetent to your employees.

2. Compromising

This means trying to come up with a solution that satisfies some but not all of the concerns expressed by the arguing team members. You are asking each to give up some of their needs to find a middle ground. This may seem like a lose-lose situation as both sides have to concede something. This style is best used when seeking a temporary solution or trying to defuse a conflict that seems stuck. At that point, any solution is better than none. Although both people may not like it, sometimes compromising is the only way out of the quagmire.

The benefit of compromising is that issues can be decided swiftly and those involved may gain a better understanding of the other's perspective. It may also make collaboration easier in the future. As a manager, you will come off as being a hands-on problem-solver. However, one side may feel short-changed, leading them to reject compromise in future conflicts. Overly relying on this style of conflict management could cost you goodwill with your employees.

3. Competing

This style focuses on satisfying one person's concerns without considering the other side at all. It is used by headstrong people who don't want to compromise in any way. I would suggest only using the competing style when you're standing up for your principles or when everything else you've tried has failed.

As a manager, this style helps you project strength and show you're not willing to compromise your principles. It ensures quick resolution of disputes since there is no room for negotiation. However, don't rely on this style too often. You may come across as unreasonable and dictatorial. Your employees may not be happy and productivity may decline.

4. Accommodating

This style is the opposite of competing, as you try to satisfy someone else's concerns ahead of your own. You should use this style when you know you have wronged the other party and there's no need to argue. It is also appropriate when the issue at hand isn't of much concern to you and you just want to maintain the peace. For example, you can be accommodating when selecting colors to use in a new ad campaign.

Accommodating may be the best option for quickly resolving a small disagreement. But it is not the style to use when dealing with major issues.

As a manager, your employees will view you as easy to work with. It also gives employees confidence to speak their minds without fear of repercussions. On the other hand, you may appear weak if you are too often accommodating. This is not the style to use when dealing with major issues.

5. Collaborating

This style focuses on finding a win-win solution where everyone is happy with the outcome. It is used when relationships are important and solutions have a major impact. All interests must be considered if the conflict is to be resolved. For example, two team members want to implement different design features for a project.

They decide to sit down, explore each feature and then incorporate a combination of features from both designs. By working together, they reach an effective solution.

Collaborating is the most appropriate style for long-term results. It is the sweet spot between being assertive while still seeking to fully cooperate with the other party. Everyone is happy and the problem is solved. As the manager, you are seen as a skilled negotiator. Keep in mind, though, that this style takes hard work, honest communication, and openness to be effective.

CONFLICT RESOLUTION ASSESSMENT

As you read through the above conflict management styles, which do you think suits you best? Which one have you been using so far? It's incredibly helpful to understand the style you naturally use as a leader. You can also use this information to create an assessment to determine how your employees manage their conflicts.

A conflict management quiz is a series of questions designed to rate how often you take a specific action. There are about 15 to 30 questions, and each question is rated on a scale of 1 to 5. The results can help you determine if you need to undergo conflict management training.

Also, if you're interviewing potential employees, you can use a conflict management quiz to identify how they deal with conflict. This will let you know who utilizes an effective approach and which ones need to work on their conflict management skills.

Conflict management quiz

In the quiz below, several statements are used to describe potential behavioral responses. For each question, rate how often you take the action specified. Use a rating of 1 to 5.

1. *During an argument, I avoid the situation as fast as possible.*
2. *During a conflict, I talk to all parties to find the best solution.*
3. *I enjoy meeting the other party halfway.*
4. *I argue my position until the other party concedes because I know the best solution.*
5. *I'd rather maintain peace than argue my point.*
6. *I rarely bring up contentious issues and keep disagreements to myself.*
7. *I love engaging in and winning disagreements.*
8. *I go out of my way to see all sides of a disagreement and understand the issues involved.*

9. *I often negotiate to try and find common ground in a conflict.*
10. *I prefer to keep communicating with the other party in a disagreement to find an amicable solution.*
11. *I get anxious during disagreements, so I try my best to minimize them,*
12. *I will keep arguing until the other party accepts defeat.*
13. *I feel that arguing is useless, so I agree with whatever others say.*
14. *I hate conflicts. I would rather fix the problem and spend time working on other things.*
15. *I always try to recognize and meet people's expectations.*
16. *I try to show the other party why my opinion is logical and beneficial.*
17. *I always ask for the other party's help to find a solution.*
18. *I seek an intermediate position.*
19. *I feel that it's not important to worry about differences.*
20. *Instead of focusing on things we don't agree on, I emphasize the things we both agree on.*
21. *I prefer to allow others to take responsibility for fixing problems.*
22. *I am willing to give up some of my opinions in exchange for others.*

23. *I try to get all contentious issues out in the open as quickly as possible.*
24. *I assert my views and desires in every disagreement.*
25. *I don't want the other person's feelings to get hurt.*

Tips

- Questions 1, 6, 11, 19 and 21 represent an avoidant style.
- Questions 5, 13, 15, 20 and 25 represent an accommodating style.
- Questions 3, 9, 14, 18 and 22 represent a compromising style.
- Questions 4, 7, 12, 16 and 24 represent a competing style.
- Questions 2, 8, 10, 17 and 23 represent a collaborative style.

When you've completed the quiz, add up the scores for each style. This will reveal the ones you naturally rely on in a conflict. Keep in mind that you are not exclusively oriented to only one style. You may often use a range of styles in your conflicts. However, you may be overusing one or two particular styles. Some are not as effective as others, and you shouldn't use them as often. If you rely too heavily on the weaker styles (i.e., competing, compromising, and avoiding), you may need additional conflict management training.

CHAPTER TAKEAWAYS

Learning conflict management skills will help you prepare for any conflict situation whether it's personal or professional. Next, let's talk about how you can use the power of your personality in conflict management.

4

HOW YOUR PERSONALITY SHAPES YOUR CONFLICT MANAGEMENT STYLE

In the previous chapter, we talked about five conflict management styles. If you examine these styles keenly, you'll notice each one is related to personality. For example, if you predominantly adopt a competing conflict management style, you're likely to have a direct and controlling personality. If you usually rely on an avoidant style, you're probably casual and a conformist. In other words, your innate personality helps shape your conflict management style.

You also learned your style is not set in stone. You can change how you manage conflict personally and professionally regardless of your personality. But before you can undergo effective conflict management training, you should gain a deeper understanding of how your personality affects how you handle conflict.

This insight will give you a more holistic foundation for your conflict management style.

This chapter covers tools and models to help you understand your personality and its corresponding behaviors. You will learn about different personality types and how to work with color energies to grow and improve your personal and professional relationships.

WHAT IS INSIGHTS DISCOVERY?

Insights Discovery is a methodology based on Carl Jung's psychological principles. It uses a simple, yet memorable four-color model to help you understand your personality and other associated behaviors. This tool is used by businesses and individuals to improve self-awareness, decision-making, communication and performance.

It involves an online evaluation process where you spend about 20 minutes answering comprehensive multiple-choice questions. When you complete the evaluation, an in-depth personal profile is generated. The profile reveals your strengths, weaknesses as well as how you approach problems, your preferred communication style and the value you bring to a team.

An Insights Discovery profile uses four colors to represent your personality preferences. These colors are

Cool Blue, Earth Green, Sunshine Yellow and Fiery Red. Your profile will use these colors to reveal specific traits about you. By identifying this unique color mix, you gain a better understanding of your inner motivations, thoughts and actions. This can serve as a powerful guide on how to work more effectively with others, especially when it comes to conflicts.

Ready to dive in?

UNDERSTANDING THE INSIGHTS COLOR ENERGIES

Here is a basic breakdown of what the colors mean in terms of your personality.

Cool Blue

You are cautious, precise, deliberate, questioning and formal in your approach to life. You prefer to be correct over being liked. You make decisions that are deliberate and logical, making you a natural problem-solver. You fear public embarrassment and when put under pressure; you tend to withdraw. You don't get along with others who are careless or vague in their work, so you prefer the company of precise people.

Earth Green

You are caring, encouraging, patient and relaxed. People see you as casual and conforming. You want others to like you so you tend to share a lot. Your main goal is to maintain harmony, so you prefer to be around pleasant people. You hate and avoid confrontation and are irritated by impatient or insensitive people. You make decisions after careful consideration and often feel overburdened under pressure.

Sunshine Yellow

You are social, enthusiastic, dynamic and persuasive. Others perceive you as being informal and preferring to hang out with fun people. Your main desire is to be admired which makes you fear disapproval. You hate being constrained by rules and routines and love-making spontaneous decisions. When under pressure, you tend to overreact and become dramatic.

Fiery Red

You are demanding, competitive, strong-willed, purposeful and determined. You appear to be very functional and business-like. Being in control of yourself and others is something you like to do. Your primary focus is on pragmatism and results. This means you prefer those around you to be brief and direct. You get irritated when you see indecisiveness and inefficiency. When placed under pressure, you tend to become dictatorial.

HOW TO WORK WITH COLOR ENERGIES

Do you recognize your color energy? Maybe you thought about your family, friends and colleagues and tried to identify their color energies, too. Recognizing your colors helps you learn how to adapt your behavior to meet the needs of others.

Whether at home or in the office, you are always interacting with others. It's important to know how to interact with the other person's color energy to create a deeper connection. This can also help you prevent or resolve conflicts quickly and effectively.

In this section, let's assume you're a team manager about to have a performance review with a member of your team. They have been underperforming for a while and it's time to resolve the issue. You have already identified their color energy and now you want to use that information to deliver performance feedback. The information below can help you shape your critique respectfully and effectively.

Red energy

You are dealing with a direct and pragmatic person so keep the meeting formal and business-like. Prepare clear objectives to help you stay on target. Don't be afraid to share your views and get to the point as quickly as possible. Detail areas where they are underperforming and explain how their performance is linked to their success in the organization

Yellow energy

This is someone who loves to talk so ensure there's enough time to chat about a lot of topics. If possible, hold the meeting in a casual or informal setting like a coffee shop. During the discussion, use clear examples to explain where they are underperforming. Use stories and even humor to paint a broader picture for them. Acknowledge and praise their good performance in other areas but don't let them blame others for their failures.

Green energy

This colleague is caring, harmonious and hates confrontation so conduct the meeting in a comfortable and relaxed place. Avoid talking across a desk. A quiet and private talk over coffee is better. Don't expect them to agree with your perspective after only one meeting. Remember, this is someone who makes decisions slowly and hates pressure. You might give them information ahead of the meeting so they can think about how they will respond. As you explain their underperformance, ask them to consider the impact of their work on the team or organization. Don't rush the conversation and do give them time to respond. Avoid blaming them or saying something insensitive as they may shut down.

Blue energy

This individual is highly analytical. If you're going to claim they are underperforming, you better have the facts to back it up. You should come to the meeting with logical evidence and clear examples. Write down the agenda and share it before the meeting. You should meet somewhere formal that displays professionalism and order. State your case, don't waste time on frivolous matters. You should also allow for silent intervals as they reflect on what to say.

COLOR ENERGIES AND HOW THEY HANDLE STRESS

Without a doubt, learning about color energies can help you better connect with others. But this is only possible in a calm situation. So what happens when you or someone else is under stress and things get out of control? If this occurs in the workplace, you or your colleagues may behave inappropriately.

Let's assume you're a team leader and a stressful event has just occurred. A team member is behaving disorderly, and you need to remedy the situation. Identify how to handle the situation in a specific way depending on their color energy. Once you know how to recognize stress triggers and signals for the different energies, you will know the best solutions to reduce workplace disruption.

Fiery Red energy

People with this color energy are triggered by others who are indecisive and unfocused. They also get stressed when they are not in control of outcomes. You will know they are under stress when they start being impatient, aggressive and demanding. To remedy the situation, allow the person to make quick decisions, take a time out or have a measure of control over the task.

Sunshine Yellow energy

Those with this color energy are triggered by personal rejection, lack of fun interactions and too many restrictions. When stressed, they become argumentative, opinionated and overly responsive. To remedy the situation, give the team member more flexibility or distract them with a different task.

Earth Green energy

People with this color energy are triggered by a violation of their values, unfair treatment or being forced to hurry. When stressed, they become silent and withdrawn. They may also be stubborn, judgmental and impersonal to their teammates. The best thing to do is reach out to them personally to restore their trust. You can also reschedule the task or push the deadline back.

Cool Blue energy

Those with this color energy are stressed out by lack of information, poor work quality, wasting time or being asked to rush. When stressed, they nitpick, become resentful and start asking too many questions. They may even withdraw or become aloof. To fix the situation, ask for their feedback or go back and analyze the work with greater care. Provide more information and emotional support to draw them back into the team.

BENEFITS OF THE INSIGHTS DISCOVERY MODEL

One of the biggest advantages of the Insights Discovery model is its accessibility. The color scheme is easy to understand and identify in your everyday behaviors. It also helps you understand the behaviors of those around you. The model is easy to remember, enabling you to quickly associate a particular behavior and its corresponding color. And this makes it easier to focus on improving yourself and others around you.

It is also extremely useful for executing organizational change and solving business challenges. It can help assess an organization's management and employees when undertaking leadership changes or team restructuring. This is a great tool to better identify organizational culture and improve customer service.

Consider using the four-color model in the Insights Discovery profile as a universally accepted language used to serve an organization's unique business needs. Employees become more self-aware and find it easier to talk openly about challenges, team strengths and weaknesses, and areas of improvement. It provides you with a better way to understand your colleagues and the best way to communicate with them.

The color energies help identify potential sources of conflict between members on the same team. For example, a fiery red personality may clash with an earth green personality because one is too dominant over the other. On the other hand, individuals who share the same or similar color energies may not be very productive working together. For example, too many cool blues in one team may lead to getting stuck on details. The solution to these personality imbalances is to focus on creating a natural harmony rather than an artificial one.

Let's consider this example.

You are a team leader in charge of a team of three employees. You tend to lead from a fiery red color while the others each have another color energy. Your team is tasked with integrating a new remote work software that has been introduced into the organization. The software will improve collaboration and performance, but your manager has put the project on a tight deadline. As a fiery red personality, you tend to be demanding, even dictatorial, when under pressure. Since you've studied color energies, you understand how to approach team members according to their color energy. You want to get the best out of everyone without creating unnecessary conflict. How do you go about doing this?

When handling a member with high dominant sunshine yellow, give them tasks that are flexible and don't require much structure. Talk to them often and use stories to illustrate what you want them to achieve. Offer them praise to encourage them to work hard. You may need to micromanage them to prevent them from slacking off.

When handling a member with a high dominant cool blue, use a structured approach such as diagrams and a lot of written instructions to guide them. Frame the project as a problem that needs to be solved and give them the tools to solve it. As long as your instructions are clear and precise, you won't need to micromanage them.

When handling a member with a high dominant earth green, share the inspiration behind the project. Explain how the new software will benefit everyone and improve collaboration in the company. Give them task instructions in advance so they can think things through before the project starts. Offer them encouragement and provide a relaxed atmosphere to motivate them to perform well.

CHAPTER TAKEAWAYS

As you can see, the Insights Discovery color energies are useful for understanding yourself, your behaviors and the way you perceive the world around you. They enable you to engage with others in a more holistic and empathetic way rather than the judgmental manner we tend to perceive each other. Though color energies are a great and easy-to-use tool, there are some basic dos and don'ts you need to know. These guidelines will help you use the tool in a fair and balanced way as you apply them to yourself and others.

Do:

1. Remember everyone is a combination of all four colors and not just one.
2. Look at individuals holistically since many other factors may influence their choices.
3. Be careful to separate your opinions from facts.
4. Understand that some individuals are exceptions to the rule.
5. Remember that this model describes an individual's preferences and not their skill or intelligence.

Don't:

1. Ever put anyone in a box!
2. Belittle others because of their color energy spread.
3. Use your color spread as an excuse to avoid learning or doing particular tasks.
4. Tell someone what you think their color spread should be before they take the quiz for themselves.

5. Assume an individual cannot transcend their behavioral preference through education or experience.

As a leader, you can use these color energies and personalities to create a team that stimulates constructive conflict. If you do this correctly, you'll find it easier to get through the phases of any conflict that arises. Next, let's talk about the different phases of conflict from the moment it arises to its resolution.

5

THE PHASES OF CONFLICT MANAGEMENT

From what we've talked about so far, you may think that the process of managing and resolving conflicts is straightforward. You may even think it is an absolute fix for any situation. But this isn't always the case. You can prepare to face a confrontation, whether in your personal or professional life, but something goes wrong, and you're caught off guard. You thought a conflict would go one way but ended up going in the opposite direction.

This happens because conflicts tend to trigger strong emotions. In most cases, these emotions are strongly negative and can lead to discomfort, disappointment and hurt feelings. If the conflict is managed well, it leads to greater understanding, deeper trust and stronger relationships. But if you fail to manage conflicts properly, your emotions can cloud your judgment. This may lead to resentment, irreparable rifts and even a breakup of the relationship.

When emotions cloud your judgment, something that seems right or logical may simply be a bias. So, it's really important to take a methodical and precise approach to manage conflict. Don't worry, this doesn't have to be difficult! Conflict management can be achieved quite easily without creating much confusion. There is a four-phase process that can help you deal with conflict in every situation and with every person.

This process provides a dynamic understanding of all the other parties involved in the conflict—including you. It allows you to take a deeper look at the various aspects of conflict management, including active listening, using empathy to evaluate individuals, promoting collaboration and taking action on the plan you've created.

Next, I'm going to lay out a four-stage hack I created to help you manage and resolve conflicts effectively. It is a clear and easy-to-follow guide that contains general information about how to handle all kinds of conflict. We'll dig into each of these four phases in the next few chapters.

THE FOUR PHASES OF MANAGING CONFLICT

In Chapter One, we discussed the nature of conflict and the phases it goes through. Every conflict follows a specific pattern that begins with a misunderstanding caused by several factors, such as limited resources, unmet needs or differences in values. If the misunderstanding isn't resolved effectively and quickly, it can trigger a disagreement that spirals into an extended conflict.

You can prevent a disagreement from turning into a full-blown conflict by understanding the phases that conflict goes through. This knowledge can help you anticipate the potential effects of the conflict, enabling you to use appropriate measures to manage it. Once you reach this point, it's time to put your knowledge of conflict management and the phases to work for you.

There are four phases in conflict management. They are a step-by-step approach to help you deal with conflict from the moment it arises to its final resolution. These are: handling disagreements, creating mutual understanding, focusing on shared goals and taking action.

Phase 1: Handle the disagreement

When a conflict arises, the first thing you might want to do is launch yourself into the fray and act to resolve it. First, consider creating a safe and conducive environment so the conflict can remain stable and well-tempered. The environment must support constructive conflict to encourage everyone to express themselves freely. Your employees must feel safe to openly participate, raise issues and voice their displeasure.

Your goal? To create an environment that allows for conflicts to be handled properly without triggering unnecessary emotional problems. Negative emotions tend to disrupt trust, prevent effective communication and make the issue at hand harder to resolve. Since you can't control other people's emotions, start by calming yourself. Don't let the heat of the moment influence your thoughts and actions.

Getting your emotions under control is an important step because anger and stress can cause you to say something you might regret. Your emotions may trickle into the argument and you'll likely end up speaking more than listening. If the other person says something critical, you may not be able to take it calmly.

As a leader, you want to display level-headedness and patience in conflict situations. Anger isn't a good way to get people to listen or do what you say. Avoid handling a confrontation while angry. That could intimidate the other party to submit in the short term or it could lead them to plot behind your back. If you're feeling emotional and need to calm down, take a walk or engage in physical activity to clear your head. Once you've released your negative emotions, go back and act immediately to resolve the conflict. You want to avoid the temptation to let it linger for too long.

As you handle the conflict, ensure you're actively listening to what others are saying. Active listening requires you to have an open mind. Pay attention to the phrases the other person is using, then respond using the same phrasing. This shows them you are listening and also helps clarify any confusion over the issues. Also, pay attention to their body language. Nonverbal cues such as tone of voice, body posture and facial expressions can help you spot sentiments they might be trying to hide.

Active listening and reading body language are important in this phase of the conflict management process. As you keep your ears and eyes open, accept any negative feedback that may come your way. Validate and acknowledge the root cause of their emotions even if they are negative. If you find yourself in a conflict with someone who has highly charged emotions, be patient and practice emotional intelligence. Be considerate and find ways to lower these emotions immediately to maintain a good relationship moving forward.

And finally, create fair ground rules for everyone. This is especially important if you are handling a conflict that involves more than two people.

Phase 2: Create mutual understanding

At this point of the conflict, everyone has already put forth their opinions. Now it's time to tap deeper into their wants and needs, as well as your own. Keep in mind the conflict is due to some kind of disagreement. People disagree because they want different things. Figuring out what they want makes it easier for you to create mutual understanding. How do you achieve this? The best way is to use empathy, active listening and the right questions.

During the conflict, you should use empathy to help you see and understand what others want. Empathy is like a bridge connecting you to the thoughts and emotions of others, especially when combined with active listening. You already used active listening in the previous phase, so channel it again to help you better understand all parties involved. As you do, validate their pain and problems and assure them you are seriously considering everything they've said.

Active listening is a huge part of any meaningful interaction. Unfortunately, it's often overlooked when resolving conflicts. Since people can't wait to interrupt the other person, they aren't truly paying attention to what's being said. You may be tempted to jump in during the conversation to explain every little detail of your side. You may feel like you have to try your best to convince the other side to agree with your opinion. Don't let yourself fall into this trap! The temporary satisfaction you'll get from airing your views won't be worth it in the long run.

Allow the other person to speak uninterrupted. You may be surprised to discover you misunderstood their original point and the entire conflict is not about what you thought it was. At this point, frame questions to help you understand what the other party wants. As you listen and read their body language, ask questions to clarify any points that aren't clear to you. Stating it aloud also helps the other party clarify their intentions and goals.

Don't forget to ask yourself what you want to happen to resolve the conflict. Take some time to think about why you're having this conversation with yourself.

"What concerns do I have about the relationship?", "What do I want the other party to know?", "What are my desired goals for this discussion?" Asking the right questions can help you set clear intentions about what you want to achieve at the end of this conversation. These questions make it easier to decide on the tone of the meeting, what needs to be said and what needs to be left out of the conversation.

Phase 3: Focus on shared goals

Now that everyone has identified and understood each other's needs and goals, the focus should shift to finding shared goals. Both parties need to find common ground if they want to continue working toward. If both parties have a win-win perspective, it will be easier to figure out a solution that works well for everyone. The key to finding shared goals is to focus on interests instead of positions. Start by identifying the compatible and incompatible issues between the two sides. Then let each person list and prioritize their goals. This will help each side know how to trade out unimportant goals for the sake of finding common ground on more important issues.

As you try to find shared goals, don't forget to create an atmosphere of positivity and goodwill. This will allow everyone to feel free to continue sharing their thoughts and feelings. If nobody is happy about the way the conflict is being handled, it becomes much harder to agree on a solution. Even when someone does compromise on an issue, their half-hearted approach won't guarantee they will follow through on the agreement. An environment without goodwill only provides people with an excuse to shut down and not deal with the conflict. Positivity ensures the conversation keeps moving forward and puts everyone involved at ease.

Despite attempts to maintain a positive attitude, a conflict sometimes can get heated, and people end up saying things they shouldn't. A brief moment of madness may be enough to burn the bridge that connects two people. So, it's important to always keep in mind the need to preserve a relationship you care about. Don't forget to focus on the bigger picture. Remember that resolving the conflict isn't the only priority here. If you intend to work or cohabit with the person, you must prioritize being considerate and mindful.

Show your consideration for the other person by being respectful at all times. It might be tempting but avoid the temptation to jump on the offensive or use a rude tone. Don't point fingers or blame others for your actions. And avoid sharing sensitive details with those who aren't directly involved. For example, if it's a work-related conflict, there's no need to gossip with a co-worker in a similar role or a subordinate. Doing so may offend the other party in the conflict. If you need to talk to someone, consult a superior or someone outside the organization.

Another way to show consideration and keep the discussion's forward momentum is to ask questions instead of drawing assumptions. It's often easier to simply ask a question instead of assuming something that could stall the conflict resolution process. Also make sure everyone has enough time to express themselves. If the discussion becomes heated and you become the aggressor, apologize for losing your cool and try to stay focused on the issues rather than personalities. Apologizing isn't easy but you must be willing to swallow your pride and make amends. If the other party was offensive, forgive them after they've apologized.

Of course, there are times when forgiveness is not enough to resolve the issues that triggered the conflict. If you've been trying to resolve a conflict and there's no way to settle it without damaging the relationship, it might be time to consider other options. Sometimes The conflict can't be resolved and you need to walk away. It's a tough decision, but going separate ways may be what both parties need. If separating is an option, just make sure that all involved forgive, forget and move on in peace.

But if you want to stick it out in hopes of preserving a relationship, there's always the option of involving an outside facilitator. A mediator is a good choice if you feel you can't handle the conflict on your own. Mediators provide valuable help, especially in situations where the parties are overwhelmed by emotions. A mediator will gain the parties' trust, manage the hostilities, create solutions and ensure everyone commits to a solution. A mediator can also control the flow of communication between all parties, ensuring everyone stays respectful and courteous. Mediators also seek out any areas where both sides agree to help create common ground.

Phase 4: Take action

Once both sides have put forward their ideas, opinions and needs, the next step is to find the problem's root cause. This means separating the individual from the problem. It's difficult to get to the bottom of a conflict if both sides are busy pointing fingers and hurling personal insults. Instead, focus on diagnosing the conflict's cause so you can create effective solutions to help prevent future conflicts.

Creating effective solutions means developing an action plan to effectively deal with underlying issues. Each action generates a reaction, so consider what these outcomes may be. A good way to understand where your actions will lead is to create a cause-and-effect diagram. This is a graphical tool that shows the factors contributing to a specific problem. By studying the diagram, you can avoid taking actions that may harm one or both parties in the conflict.

To find solutions that will work for everyone, brainstorm ideas that bring the conflict closer to a resolution. Any options in your action plan must help promote the ideas you've brainstormed. During the brainstorming session, try not to judge others' opinions and ideas, stifling creativity and risking offense. Once you've brainstormed as many options as possible, you can evaluate them based on whether they work for everyone. Any ideas that don't promote everybody's goals should be crossed off the list.

Focus on ideas that are mutually beneficial and cause minimal harm to both sides. And you want everyone to work together to come up with multiple ways to create a solution. As you lead them to collaborate, find ways to encourage a sense of trust in each other. Negotiations are easier if both sides trust each other and believe in finding a fair solution for all involved.

And if you didn't complete Phase 3 (i.e., failed to find any common ground), you should continue the brainstorming process. Keep talking and developing new ideas to better understand where the other party is coming from. Don't give up prematurely, especially if both sides are serious about finding a win-win scenario to the conflict.

It can be easy to jump on your first idea, but you want to come up with as many options as possible on how to solve the problem. For every option you come up with, find alternatives suitable for both parties. They will act as a backup in case the initial idea fails to work. And don't forget to assess the chances of success for each option. Once both sides are comfortable with the options and alternatives, take all the ideas you've gathered so far and build solutions that work for everyone. Evaluate every solution to ensure they fit personal goals, shared goals and the compromises both sides have agreed on.

Finally, develop an action plan to implement the solutions agreed upon. It helps if there is a level of accountability to ensure both sides follow through on the plan. Consider holding regular meetings to check the plan's progress and then fine-tuning any areas that need an adjustment. The meetings can also ensure any deadlines agreed upon are on track.

CHAPTER TAKEAWAYS

Emotional awareness is a key trait in every phase of conflict management. It shows how conscious you are of the emotions of others as well as your own. But how well *are* you in tune with your emotions? Try out this short quiz to help you assess your level of emotional awareness. Don't worry, there's no correct or incorrect response. Simply answer with "almost always," "very often," "often," "occasionally" or "almost never."

- *Do your emotions play a role in your decision-making?*
- *Do you experience emotions that are intense enough to grab your attention and that of other people?*
- *Do you experience emotions that flow one after another from moment to moment?*
- *Do you experience diverse emotions (such as joy, anger and fear) and do you notice them in people's facial expressions?*
- *Do physical symptoms (for example, in your chest or stomach) accompany your emotions?*

We've talked about the four phases of conflict management. They provide a clear path to resolve any conflict. But the information in this chapter is broad and doesn't go into details. In the next four chapters, we'll be exploring each phase in greater detail so you can understand how to execute their critical aspects. Let's look at the first phase: how to handle a disagreement when it initially arises.

PHASE I – HOW TO HANDLE DISAGREEMENTS

In the previous chapter, we discussed the four phases of conflict management. The first phase dealt with handling the disagreement when it first arose. When a disagreement flares up, people are often engaged in a debate about a particular topic, usually something they all care about. This is why the conversation can easily turn into an argument. Everyone believes they are right and the others are wrong, so they invest a lot of emotional energy into the argument.

And if you invest a lot of emotion into something and then encounter resistance, you're likely to lose your cool. You become overwhelmed by negative feelings such as fear, anxiety, stress and frustration. In your mind, the only way to achieve our objective is to eliminate the resistance. So it makes sense that anyone who doesn't agree with you becomes an enemy to be destroyed. You end up relying on destructive emotions and behaviors such as anger, arrogance, insults and even threats.

The problem with such outbursts is that you end up triggering a similar reaction in the other person. Now you have a situation where both sides are worked up, nobody is listening to the other and everybody is being controlled by negative emotions. The result is a conflict that cannot progress to a mutually beneficial conclusion unless someone intervenes.

Someone needs to intervene who knows how to work with both sides of the conflict. You must calm both sides, get them to listen to one another and establish guidelines on how the conflict will be resolved. This chapter covers some key techniques to help you stay calm during conflict. You will learn about active listening and the steps to be an effective communicator. And you'll also learn how to create ground rules that enforce a positive environment for conflict resolution.

LEARNING TO STAY CALM

You walk into the office and the first person you see is the colleague you disagreed with the day before. A lump forms in your throat - you dread facing them again. A bead of sweat rolls down your forehead as your palms become clammy. At that moment, all you want to do is disappear, rush to the bathroom, and pull yourself together.

This scenario happens all the time - I bet it's happened to you, too. The bottom line is that everyone has experienced a moment when they were unable to appear cool, calm and collected. Sometimes you may be unable to focus on your work or be a productive member of a team.

This inability to focus when upset is due to a loss of access to your prefrontal cortex. When you feel threatened, your fight-or-flight instinct kicks in and triggers shortness of breath and an elevated heart rate. All rational thinking goes out the window and you either flee from the conflict or become hyper-aggressive toward the other person. None of these are ideal for dealing with conflict. So let's look at some strategies you can use to stay calm throughout a conflict.

Strategy 1: Pay attention to early warning signals

Signs such as a racing heartbeat, shaking hands and sweaty palms all indicate you are beginning to get agitated. Apart from these general ones, you may have your own unique signals. Identify your warning signals and their triggers so you can excuse yourself from a tense situation early on. Use that time to calm down before re-engaging in the confrontation.

Strategy 2: Avoid raising your voice

Resist raising your voice just because the other person has said something aggravating. It's worth taking a few deep breaths before responding, to help maintain your calm.

Strategy 3: Listen

There are instances where a misunderstanding arises due to not listening to the other person. Instead of listening, you tend to cut them off to defend yourself. By actively listening to what someone is saying, you can understand their perspective and respond accordingly. This shows you care about their feelings and genuinely want to resolve the issue.

Strategy 4: Fight fair

If someone accuses you of doing something wrong, focus on the issue and resolve it. This isn't the time to bring up information you've been holding for months, waiting to unleash it at the right moment. Resorting to unfair tactics will only confuse issues and open up new conflicts.

Strategy 5: Think before you speak

Before you engage in a serious conversation with someone, consider the best timing and location for it. If you confront your colleague and accuse them in front of everyone in the break room, they are likely to respond aggressively to avoid embarrassment. Instead, consider confronting them privately at a time when you can both stay calm.

Strategy 6: Don't ask someone why they are freaking out

Asking someone why they are freaking out when they are clearly upset can only have one outcome. They're going to get even more upset, and this will make the situation worse. Instead, acknowledge how they feel and agree to have a peaceful conversation soon, to settle any issues.

Strategy 7: Create your conflict mantra

Have you used a mantra before? It's a phrase you mentally repeat to help you focus. You can create a conflict mantra to remind you that conflict is normal and not a life-and-death situation. For example, you can say, "Conflict makes me stronger," "I can overcome this" or "Conflict can't hurt me."

Strategy 8: Create a go-to script

When someone unexpectedly calls you out for poor work performance, you're likely to feel flustered and at a loss for words. Being tongue-tied may make you look bad in front of others. So create a go-to response for those moments when you are caught unaware by a sudden confrontation. Your go-to script can be as simple as "I see your point. Can we sit down and find a solution that works for both of us?" This will give you time to compose yourself and think of a more detailed response.

Strategy 9: Don't worry about how you look

There are physical signs you usually show when you are uncomfortable or anxious. It could be sweaty hands, rosy cheeks or even a trembling lip. Most people think their signs of discomfort are visible to everyone, but they usually aren't so obvious. If you keep worrying about how you look to others, your worry can exacerbate your signs of anxiety. Don't worry about your sweaty hands, because no one is likely to notice.

Strategy 10: Adopt some breathing techniques

Some simple breathing hacks can help you stay calm during tense conversations. When you take deep, slow breaths, you stop your body from going into a reactive mode. Deep breathing can help trigger your parasympathetic nervous system which calms you down. Inhale for a count of four, then exhale for the same number of four counts. You can also use the 4-7-8 method where you inhale for four counts, hold your breath for seven counts and exhale for eight counts. Other simple hacks include relaxing your shoulders and jaw.

Strategy 11: Adopt a win-win perspective

Although this may seem difficult during an argument, it's an effective way to avoid making a tense situation worse. So focus on the bigger picture and what the relationship means to you. If you want to maintain it, look for a win-win outcome. Even if it's a serious argument, see the conflict as a passing event that won't matter a year from now. If you can find a way to work together, everyone ends up satisfied with the outcome.

Strategy 12: Separate yourself psychologically from the event

When you're in a conflict situation, the worst thing you can do is allow your emotions to spiral out of control. If you're flustered, find a way to psychologically separate yourself from whatever is upsetting you. You could recall a happy memory such as watching a sunset with a loved one. Or pretend to be a fly on the wall observing the situation. Another effective strategy is to concentrate on the physical environment around you such as the feeling of the fabric on the chair you're sitting on.

Strategy 13: Disrupt your stress response

Conflict tends to create a stress response in the body. If unchecked, that response may trigger a flood of negative emotions that cloud your judgment. To regain control of your mind and body, it helps to recognize your thoughts and emotions. Name the emotion, then separate yourself from it. Secondly, accept the emotion, as a way to practice self-compassion. Thirdly, investigate the emotion and how it makes your body feel. Is it a pleasant feeling? Is it a sinking feeling? Does it motivate you to act? Finally, take time to nurture yourself after the stress response. If you start to feel stressed because someone accuses you, excuse yourself and tell them you need time to think over the issue. Then you can take a walk, do yoga or meditate. When you've calmed down, you can go back and have the conversation.

Strategy 14: Defend yourself

Defend yourself by being assertive. This is more effective in bringing a conflict to a resolution than being passive or hostile. Be prepared to defend yourself. Don't let the other person push you around. State your position clearly and be honest about how you feel.

Respectfully ask for what you need to let the other person understand your perspective.

Strategy 15: Do what you can

If the situation doesn't allow you to step away to compose yourself, you have to do what you can and engage in the conversation there and then. This especially applies to situations where you're talking to an angry client or boss. Do your best to pacify them by maintaining a low and measured tone of voice. This will alert your body to stay calm. And when the other person notices you're composed and relaxed, they will mirror your response and calm down. This is likely to defuse the tense situation. Also, avoid interrupting them as this could make them more agitated.

Strategy 16: Agree to disagree

Some conflicts can't be resolved, and you just have to agree to disagree. Remove yourself from the argument instead of getting stuck in endless cycles that aren't achieving anything. If necessary, involve a third party such as the HR manager or a professional counselor.

THE IMPORTANCE OF ACTIVE LISTENING

We've all been in arguments at some point in our lives. When you're arguing, you feel compelled to defend your viewpoint at all costs. It doesn't matter what the other person says. You go all out to counter whatever narrative they present. The more intense the argument, the more energy you put into disagreeing. You're not interested in understanding their perspective. You just want to win the argument.

This need to win is the conundrum most people find themselves in during an argument. Everyone wastes their time talking over each other rather than listening. Which totally defeats the point of arguing - exchanging ideas, listening to each other and understanding where the other person is coming from.

But there can be no understanding if both sides are too busy planning what to say next as the other person speaks. Instead of listening to the opinion being expressed, you're wracking your brain for more evidence to support your case. As a result, you fail to hear what's being said by the other person. You immediately make judgments that are unnecessarily harsh and may be damaging to the relationship.

How could you handle such a situation in a better way? The answer is active listening. This involves making a conscious effort to hear not just what someone is saying but the complete message they are communicating. It allows you to pay attention to their words and body language without being distracted by anything happening around you. You won't form counterarguments in your head or lose focus. Active listening involves acknowledging the other person's message, whether it's with a simple nod or an "uh-huh." It also means occasionally asking questions or commenting to better understand the message.

Active listening is an incredibly useful skill as an effective communicator. And it's critical when talking to someone with different opinions. Most people think there's no need to engage with someone you disagree with. But the key is to listen to their opinions. Why is this important?

Listening to those you disagree with allows you to better understand the issue. You're able to weigh the pros and cons of different opinions. This lets you learn from others and gain new ideas. Though it may be hard to listen to narratives that challenge your perceptions, you will gradually shed your fear of engaging in difficult topics. The world is full of people from diverse backgrounds who hold controversial opinions. If you don't develop the skill of actively listening to alternative voices, you'll become closed-minded and intolerant. Is it any wonder that the cancel culture is so prevalent in today's generation?

Active listening can prepare you to see the potential in people and ideas, especially now as the world strives to move forward with bold initiatives. By engaging with divergent ideas, you become a better problem-solver. Disagreements can lead to finding common ground and gaining a deeper understanding of your own beliefs. And believe it or not, those uncomfortable conversations will make you stronger than ever before.

THE STEPS TO EFFECTIVE COMMUNICATION

When we talk about effective communication, we tend to focus only on the verbal message. But communication also includes the emotions and intentions behind the message. It involves actively listening to understand the full meaning of what's being communicated.

You'd think that effective communication would be instinctive. But the truth is that when one person speaks, the message is seldom fully heard or understood. You say one thing and the other person misunderstands or hears something different. And so, most of our conflicts at work, school or in the home, begin.

To avoid these needless conflicts, focus on communicating more effectively. This will help you deepen relationships, build more trust, improve teamwork and boost your overall health. But first, you need to ask yourself, "What are some of the barriers preventing me from communicating effectively?"

Turns out, there are four factors that affect your effective communication ability. They are:

- **Stress** – This prevents you from reading other people's signals and makes you send out confusing signals to others. It makes your message off-putting and puts you in a reactive mode that might trigger a conflict.
- **Distractions** – When someone is talking to you but you're checking your phone or daydreaming, you can't clearly identify their nonverbal cues. Your lack of focus may also unintentionally send the wrong message to the other person.
- **Inconsistent body language** – Your body language should match your words. If they contradict, your listener may feel you're not being honest.
- **Negative body language** – Actions such as crossing your arms or tapping your feet are negative signals that indicate you don't like what the other person is saying. Even if you don't like the message, avoid such negative signals.

If you can avoid these barriers, you will be well on your way to becoming an effective communicator. Don't stop there, though. Next, let's consider the steps that provide you with appropriate communication skills:

Step 1: Become an active listener

To become an active listener, you need to focus fully on what the other person is saying. Focus on their words and body language to detect any subtle nuances and nonverbal signals. If you find the conversation dull, repeat the speaker's words in your head. This helps to reinforce their message and maintain your focus.

Another way to ensure you get the right message is to favor your right ear. Your right ear is connected to the left side of your brain which deals with emotions and speech comprehension. So turning your right ear toward the speaker helps you detect their subtle emotional nuances.

And if possible, avoid the urge to interrupt and share your concerns. When someone is telling you about problems with their boss, you shouldn't interrupt with your own workplace horror story. Listen carefully instead of waiting to chime in. Show you're interested in what they are saying. Nod and smile occasionally to encourage them to keep talking.

As they talk, they may say something you don't agree with. This is OK. Let them speak their mind and don't judge them for holding a different opinion. Effective communication doesn't mean you have to agree. It simply means you should understand their perspective and connect with them.

If you feel that you're disconnecting from their message, ask questions to clarify certain points. Use high-gain questions to gather as much insight as possible. You can also use reflective questions to create hypothetical scenarios that encourage the listener to self-reflect. Scaled questions such as, "How much does that bother you on a scale of 1 to 10?" can help you determine the severity of an issue. Finally, you can use hypothetical questions to help the listener visualize the future.

There are also phrases you can use to connect with a message. For example, "It sounds like you're saying …", "What do you mean by …" or "What I'm hearing is …" And if you paraphrase what the other person is saying now and again, it will ensure you understand what they mean. This lets them know you are paying attention. You will know the argument is going well when you hear them say things like, "Yes, that's what I meant" or "You're right! I think you understand my problem."

Step 2: Focus on nonverbal communication

A person's body language can tell you more about their emotional state than their words ever can. By focusing on facial expressions, gestures, posture, breathing and eye contact ,you can get a clearer picture of what they are saying. Be aware that differences in age, gender, culture and religious background can affect body language signals. Think about reading their nonverbal signals as a sum rather than focusing only on a single expression or gesture. Just because someone breaks eye contact doesn't mean you should worry. To read a person properly, focus on all their body language signals.

And don't forget that as you're reading the other person, you are also sending nonverbal signals. Make sure your body language matches your words. You should also modify your nonverbal cues according to the context. You can't address a child the same way you would talk to an adult. Consider the person's emotional state and use an appropriate tone of voice. When you're working on your own nonverbal communication, it can help to learn to manage stress and develop greater emotional awareness. Take time to calm down before engaging in a conversation. You can also use mindful meditation to increase your awareness of your emotions and how they affect you.

Step 3: Manage your stress

We previously discussed stress management as an important way to improve nonverbal communication.

This also applies to communicating effectively. Stress can make you say something during an argument that you'll later regret. This is why it's important to relieve your stress before engaging in a serious conversation.

When you notice a conversation is becoming intense, find a way to reduce stress and regulate your emotions. The first thing you can do is identify your stress signals. Pay attention to your body's responses such as shallow breathing, clenched fists or a tight stomach. Then take a moment to calm down. Take a walk, squeeze a stress ball, recall a happy memory or take some deep belly breaths. The goal is to find a technique that works for you.

Humor can also be a good way to lower stress levels. If the conversation is getting too serious, tell an amusing story to lighten the mood. You should also be willing to compromise a little to lower stress levels for both sides of the argument. Definitely consider this if the issue is more important to the other person than it is to you. At the end of the day, there's no need to stress yourself over a situation that isn't moving forward. You can agree to disagree and walk away even if it's for a short while to regain your composure.

Step 4: Be assertive

Being assertive helps you express yourself clearly, openly and honestly. You are neither passive and withdrawn nor hostile and demanding during an argument. When you assert yourself, you stand a better chance of communicating effectively and understanding the other person's point of view. How can you find that balance? Value your own opinions. You have to know your needs and openly express them even as you allow others to express theirs.

It's okay to positively express negative emotions. If you're angry, express it respectfully. If you make a mistake, apologize and learn from the experience. At the same time, set clear boundaries so others don't take advantage of you during an argument.

There are two simple techniques you can use to develop assertive communication. The first is *empathetic assertion*. This means recognizing the other person's situation before conveying your needs. For example, "I understand you're busy but I need you to complete this task by the deadline." The second technique is *escalating assertion*. You become firmer after the first technique has failed. For example, "If you don't complete this task as stipulated, I'll have to take legal action."

An effective way to be assertive in your communication is by using "I" statements rather than "You" statements. For example, instead of saying "You are always working and never have time for me," say "When you work late every day, I feel unfulfilled." Instead of saying "You never listen to me," say "When you don't listen to me, I feel frustrated." Whereas "You" statements sound accusatory and place responsibility on the listener, "I" statements place the responsibility on the speaker. These are assertive, compassionate and less hostile ways to communicate your thoughts and feelings.

EMBRACING NEGATIVE EMOTIONS

Experiencing negative emotions is a part of life. You cannot avoid or block them even if you tried. But let's face it, most people brush aside their negative emotions to avoid dealing with them. If only it was that easy! This rarely works in the long run because the underlying emotional cause is still there.

Apart from avoiding negative emotions, there is the belief that people should be positive and feel good all the time. We see this in organizations where managers go out of their way to cultivate a culture of positivity. They place a lot of emphasis on cheerleading to achieve goals or celebrate team successes. There's a deliberate effort to create a workplace where positive emotions are the norm.

But all this attention on positivity can make us forget negative emotions exist for a reason. They arise when there is an imbalance in the workplace power structure. They may also be the result of rapid and unpopular changes or an increased workload on employees. Negative emotions are not necessarily a bad thing. They can provide feedback to widen your perspective of what's happening in your environment. Negative emotions can be an opportunity to discover underlying issues bubbling under the surface for too long.

Despite these benefits, most managers view negative emotions as obstacles to be eliminated. They refuse to acknowledge such emotions in the workplace. Studies show that most executives pressure employees to hide their negative feelings. They send unhappy employees to the HR department or ask them to keep their feelings out of the workplace. Some executives believe negative emotions drain time and energy and that expressing these feelings may trigger a flood of unwelcome reactions. The result is managers clamp down on any negative sentiments from their subordinates. And this can create a chain reaction where employees are afraid to talk about their dissatisfaction. Before long, they become accustomed to ignoring their negative emotions.

Unfortunately, ignoring negative feelings only works in the short term. If they remain unresolved, it may ultimately cost the organization in terms of lost productivity, employee ineffectiveness and disengagement. When you fail to face your negative emotions, you end up blaming others for how you feel. You spend less time and energy on your work, reducing your performance and commitment to the organization.

The thing is, when you blame others, you start resenting your subordinates, colleagues and bosses. This leads to the short-circuiting of communication channels and even restricting access to resources. If things get really bad, colleagues may even unconsciously mimic the postures and facial expressions of employees who are dissatisfied and despondent. If you don't spot and deal with this in time, negative emotions may sweep through your team. Some of your best employees may leave and you might find it difficult to recruit or retain the best talent. Before this happens, step up and deal with any underlying issues in your team. Learning to embrace negative emotions can stop the tide of disengagement, dissatisfaction and poor productivity.

RESOLVING HIGHLY CHARGED CONVERSATIONS

The workplace is filled with people of diverse opinions so we already know it's inevitable there will be disagreements. And in most cases, they will be resolved peacefully. But sometimes you'll find yourself engaging in an emotionally charged situation that seems to be spiraling out of control.

So how do you handle a situation that started as a simple disagreement but transformed into a full-blown argument? Maybe you've been patient with your colleague, but they don't seem interested in calming down. The disagreement is intensifying, and you can no longer work together. What do you do?

First, don't forget that all workplace conversations exist on two levels. They are either about the task or the relationship. For example, you and a colleague are collaborating on a project. You prefer to use pie charts and bar graphs to show data during the presentation but they have a different opinion. At this point, you see the disagreement is valid because it's purely based on the task at hand. But if you and your colleague have had arguments in the past, you might assume they are opposed to your idea because they disrespect or don't trust you. The disagreement has gone beyond the task and is now about the relationship. This is when the situation can get heated.

In such a situation, it's important to separate the task from the relationship. You can use the PEARLS method to make the discussion more productive. PEARLS is an acronym for six steps to defuse an emotional conversation.

- **Partnership** – "Let's work together to complete this project."
- **Empathy** – "I feel your concern."
- **Acknowledgement** – "I see you've invested a lot of time into this idea."
- **Respect** – "I appreciate your skills and competency in this task."
- **Legitimation** – "This project would be challenging for anyone."
- **Support** – "I'm here to help you succeed in this."

Such statements can defuse a tense conversation when used well. If you feel you've overstepped a boundary, apologize so the other person feels better. Make sure you use your words to reflect genuine emotions at the appropriate time.

GROUND RULES FOR HANDLING DISAGREEMENTS

The way you handle disagreements plays a key role in whether you have satisfying relationships. If you handle conflict in a positive way, you can benefit from happy and fulfilling social connections. To handle conflicts positively, set ground rules. These are guidelines that help you deal with conflict constructively and effectively and

prevent negative communication patterns from seeping into conversations. Did you know most people don't realize that their negative verbal and nonverbal communication contribute to an escalating argument? Ground rules promote communication that is clear and productive to all involved. When communication is clear and both sides are on the same page, it is easier to find the best way to resolve the conflict. There is open respect and both parties can easily agree when and where to talk about their issues. Here are some ground rules I like to use to bring both sides together to deal with a disagreement.

- **Ground rule 1** – If the conflict escalates, there will be a time-out to talk about the disagreement. Each party will have five minutes to share their opinions and views.

- **Ground rule 2** – Each party will listen to the other thoroughly and respectfully. When one is speaking, the other will stay silent and listen.
- **Ground rule 3** – When one party is talking, no judgments or interruptions will be passed.
- **Ground rule 4** – Both parties must feel ready to move from discussing the problem to discussing solutions. They will be fair and work to achieve mutually acceptable solutions.
- **Ground rule 5** – There will be no personal attacks or insults. If one party is not ready to talk about an issue at that moment, they must choose a different time to discuss it soon.
- **Ground rule 6** – A neutral time and place will be chosen for discussions to avoid interfering with either party's personal and work schedule.

CHAPTER TAKEAWAYS

So now you know; experiencing negative emotions is normal and should be embraced, even in the workplace. Here are several things you can do to step up and deal with negative emotions if you are struggling:

- **Look in the mirror** – Develop your emotional self-awareness to identify any negative emotions that may be arising in you. Reflect on

your emotional triggers and recognize the situations or individuals that provoke you. You can also reflect on how you react to these triggers.
- **Take deep breaths** – When you feel negative emotions stirring within you, pause and take deep breaths instead of reacting to the trigger. This will help you avoid making a knee-jerk reaction that may inspire the other person to also react negatively.
- **Pay attention to body language** – Learn to read other people's body language so you can recognize when their words don't match their nonverbal behavior. You can practice by studying people at a meeting and interpreting their emotional actions. Watch for subtle signals when someone is experiencing negative emotions. This way, you'll get better at detecting negative emotions before they arise.
- **Seek out discouraged employees** – As a leader, talk to team members who seem to be struggling with negative emotions. Ask them how they are doing. As they answer, read their body language. Listen to them and pay attention to any references about feeling disappointed or discouraged.

- **Avoid fixing other people's problems** – I know it's hard, but resist the temptation to jump in and tell others how they should solve their problems. If you're a leader and an employee is dealing with negative emotions, listen to them and offer your support. Voice your concerns as lightly as possible and ask questions to help them approach the problem. If they are unwilling to accept any help, take a step back and be available if they change their mind.

The guidelines in this chapter are there to help you establish a solid foundation for settling disagreements. They ensure there's empathy, mutual respect and collaboration to resolve the conflict. Next, let's look at how to create mutual understanding between the people involved in a conflict.

PHASE II – CREATING MUTUAL UNDERSTANDING

We've looked at the first phase of conflict management—how to handle disagreements. We've discussed how to stay calm and practice active listening. These two steps are critical when faced with a disagreement that could potentially escalate into a serious conflict. We also considered how to acknowledge and deal with negative emotions as well as set ground rules for handling a disagreement.

All these steps are important in toning down tensions that may exist between those involved in the conflict. They are a means to an end because they provide you with a solid foundation to begin the process of conflict management. You can't expect to settle a conflict if the parties are engaged in a shouting match and not listening to each other. You have to channel your inner wizard and convince everyone to sit at the same table. Once that first phase is completed, you need to move them to the next phase of the process. This is the time to create a mutual understanding between the involved parties.

Now we're going to look at the importance of mutual understanding. We will explore what mutual understanding is along with some simple steps to create it. We will also discuss how to use empathy to facilitate mutual understanding and incorporate validation to find common ground and resolve conflict.

THE PATH TO MUTUAL UNDERSTANDING

A misunderstanding can occur for several reasons. The most common is a failure in communication. This can be caused by one person wrongly interpreting what the other is saying. It can happen when someone is trying to express a thought but failing to do so clearly. Maybe the other person fails to hear the message properly or understands it differently from what the speaker intended.

For example, think about two siblings arguing over an orange. They argue for hours over who should get it and why. Finally, they realize they've been arguing for nothing. One wants the orange rind to make a cake while the other wants to make orange juice. If they had talked rather than argued, they would have realized they could share the orange since each needed a separate part to achieve their objectives. It was always a win-win situation, but they were too obsessed with winning to realize it.

And we all know that a win-win situation is the best outcome for any conflict. There is a mutual gain for both parties. The most effective way to achieve this is by creating mutual understanding. The siblings could have saved time and energy by simply asking a few critical questions. There are three questions you should ask to create mutual understanding:

1. *What do I want?*

You begin by identifying what you want from the conflict. Use a positive statement to express your desire. For example, "I want to have a better relationship with my spouse" or "I want to change my work schedule." Keep in mind that what you want should be realistic for all parties involved. And if the conflict is complicated, reframe your statement into a series of steps to simplify it.

You can also separate your statement into wants and needs to make it clearer. For example, "I want to change my work schedule" is a vague way to express a want.

You can change it into a need by saying, "I need to work less than 30 hours per week." "I want to have a better relationship with my spouse" can be, "I need to spend more time on weekends with my spouse." By separating your statement into wants and needs, you create a bargaining room. Which means you're making it easier to get the solution you need out of the conflict.

2. What do they want?

After identifying your wants, you should identify what the other person wants out of the conflict. Explore their statement from all angles to maximize the possibilities for mutual gain. Try using the questions below to achieve this goal:

- *What do they want?*
- *What do they need?*
- *What do they consider to be most important?*
- *What do they consider least important?*

3. What do we want?

Once you've identified what everyone wants and needs, you should search for common ground. Use any overlap areas as starting points for creating mutual understanding. As you explore the wants and needs from both sides, determine the type of conflict you're dealing with. Is it a task conflict or a relationship conflict? As we saw in Chapter One, a task conflict is based on disagreement over a task, policies or procedures while a relationship conflict is caused by differences in personality. Knowing the type of conflict will help you identify a good starting point for resolution.

Remember, it's easier to find common ground for a task conflict rather than a relationship conflict. For example, one party may find it easier to compromise on a schedule change than if the conflict is caused by feeling disrespected. Avoid jumping to conclusions when examining your wants and needs as well as those of other parties. Dig deep to find the conflict's root cause as the issue may not be as it seems.

FACILITATING MUTUAL UNDERSTANDING THROUGH EMPATHY

One of the most fundamental skills you can develop as a leader is the ability to understand other people's emotions. This will help improve your relationships, create more productive teams and resolve conflicts. However, empathy is an interpersonal skill and most people prefer to work on their technical skills rather than connect with their emotions. Discussing your emotions or someone else's can make you feel self-conscious and ill-equipped or not confident enough to do so.

But a lack of aptitude or confidence shouldn't stop you from developing empathy. You can start by taking small steps to better understand others. Before we discuss how to develop empathy, let's define what this term means.

Empathy is your ability to identify and understand others' emotions and perspectives in a situation. Empathy gives you better insight into lifting someone's mood and offering support in challenging times. And it is one of five major aspects of emotional intelligence. Keep in mind that empathy and sympathy are not the same. Sympathy is feeling concerned but without requiring you to share the person's emotions or perspective. For example, watching someone cry evokes sympathy but not empathy because you don't know why they're in tears.

It's only after you talk to them that you can feel empathy for them. To develop empathy, you need to go through three stages—cognitive, emotional and compassionate empathy. Let's explore these stages in greater detail.

Cognitive empathy

This is your ability to rationally or intellectually understand what someone is feeling or thinking. It doesn't require emotional connection. As a leader, you might use cognitive empathy when figuring out how your team members feel so you can choose the appropriate leadership style to use. Since cognitive empathy doesn't involve emotions, some people may use it to manipulate someone emotionally vulnerable.

Emotional empathy

This is your ability to share and understand someone's feelings on a deeper level. Through emotional empathy, you use your knowledge of what the other person is feeling to create rapport. It is also referred to as "affective empathy" because it impacts your emotional state. If you're highly sensitive, someone else's pain can change your emotional state. Avoid immersing yourself too deeply into others' problems as it may damage your own emotional well-being.

This damage may come in the form of emotional burnout and can happen when you're investing too much emotion into resolving a conflict. To avoid harming yourself emotionally, take regular breaks from the resolution process to calm down. Set boundaries so the conflicting parties don't push your buttons. Emotional empathy is an important part of being a leader because it lets you build openness, honesty and trust with your team.

Compassionate empathy

This stage of empathy involves taking practical action to help the other person and reduce their pain. For example, a team member is frustrated by their poor work performance. You can acknowledge and share their pain, but you can do more by giving them practical advice on how to improve their work. Set aside time to offer guidance on how they can learn new skills, so they are better equipped for their work.

HOW TO DEVELOP EMPATHY

Your 5-year-old niece is rolling on the floor and crying because her dad told her she can't go to the fair this afternoon. She has tonsillitis and the cold weather will only make her condition worse. She runs and jumps in your lap, begging you to convince your brother to change his mind. But even after gently explaining that she's too ill and needs to rest to heal, she's still inconsolable. Although there are good reasons behind the decision to keep her home, you can still feel her disappointment and sadness.

Life brings many disappointments no matter how trivial the situation may appear. When you interact with people you care about, listen to their concerns without judging them. Let them express their feelings without dismissing them as trivial or explaining away their concerns. In the example above, you explained the reasons why your niece couldn't go to the fair, believing that she would accept them. But it would have been better to simply listen with compassion. Compassion involves being aware of another person's suffering, accepting their perspective and then taking active steps to alleviate their pain.

By accepting that suffering is universal, you can begin to seek common ground in your conflicts. When you disagree with someone, you actively listen to their side of the story. You pay attention to their body language as they communicate their needs, perceptions and prejudices. You connect with their emotions because you know empathy and compassion can help bridge your differences.

But developing empathy doesn't happen overnight. You need awareness, patience, self-accountability and dedication. This is not an easy process, and you will be tested many times. However, there are tips you can use to develop empathy, especially when resolving conflicts. Here are four things you can do:

1. Become self-aware

If you're talking to someone and feel an argument is about to erupt, what goes through your mind?

Do you become aggressive and start blaming the other person for having a contrary opinion? Are you quick to compromise even if you're in the right? Do you withdraw and avoid the conflict? Do you seek common ground? Become aware of your conflict style and accept it as a part of you. This will help you be more aware of others' natural conflict styles.

2. Consider the other perspective

Before criticizing someone's perspective, check your attitude and identify their needs and interests. Keep an open mind so you can understand where they are coming from. You may not agree with their opinion but at least show respect and acknowledge it. Ask questions to gain better insight into why they believe what they are saying.

3. Actively listen

In the previous chapter, you learned about active listening and its importance in conflict management. Paying full attention when listening to what the other party in the conflict is saying will make all the difference. Listen to the keywords and phrases they use as well as their body language. Don't interrupt and avoid disputing their opinion, justifying yourself or asking direct questions. Even if the conversation becomes uncomfortable for you, resist the urge to divert the conversation.

4. Take action

Before you take compassionate action, make sure your focus is on the other person's needs and interests. Whatever steps you take must be in their best interest. For example, if a team member seems unfocused due to a family issue, you may think telling them to work from home would be good for them. But what if coming to work offers them a respite from the pain at home? It's worth asking them what they prefer before you pitch in with advice. In the meantime, you can practice empathic actions such as smiling at others, remembering their names, being curious about them and providing constructive feedback.

PRACTICING VALIDATION AND EMPATHY

Validation means safely allowing the other person to share their thoughts and feelings without you judging or demeaning them. It shows them that their emotions matter to you even if you don't agree with what they say. As I'm sure you've seen before, most take the opposite approach in a conflict. Too many people focus on debating, belittling or attempting to change the other person's ideas and emotions. By doing this they are invalidating their opinions and beliefs just for the sake of winning an argument.

Invalidation can even go to an extreme level where you gradually manipulate the person to make them seem insane. This is known as gaslighting. When you gaslight someone, your goal is to make them doubt the reality or trick them into believing they are crazy. If you think you've never invalidated someone in this way, think again. You likely did it unintentionally without realizing the impact of your words. Here's a quick list of some invalidating statements that you've probably used or had used against you:

- *You're just being irrational.*
- *It's just a joke.*
- *You're too sensitive.*
- *Relax! Why are you freaking out?*
- *Don't be ridiculous. Why are you so emotional?*
- *That's not something to get angry over.*
- *That happened a long time ago. Get over it already!*

See how easy it is to gaslight someone without intending to? You've probably used such phrases many times at work or with your loved ones. When you say such things, you're telling the other person they don't have the right to feel the way they do. You're saying there's something wrong with them. This is not what validation looks like and is definitely not the way to resolve conflict.

WHAT DOES VALIDATION LOOK LIKE?

During a conflict, allow the other person to freely express their thoughts and feelings. Let them know it's OK to think or feel the way they do and help them feel accepted. When you validate them, you make it easier to connect with them and create an environment of trust.

Validation can be hard — we often feel like jumping in to offer advice. You become a debater or a problem solver at a time when you should be listening empathetically. You want to give the other person a piece of your mind so you can have peace of mind. It's hard enough facing your negative feelings so why deal with another person's negative emotions? The truth is that if you validate their thoughts and emotions, they typically work out their own problems in due time.

There is a quote, "People won't care how much you know until they know how much you care." Let your primary focus be to show empathy and validation before offering any kind of solution. Here are three strategies to validate a person's emotions during a conflict:

1. Repeat what you hear them saying

Reflecting on what the other person is saying is a simple, yet effective way to validate them. After they have expressed a thought or feeling, you say, "So what you're saying is …" or "It sounds like this … is extremely important to you." You can also repeat back what they've said by asking a question. For example, "So what's bothering you is that …?" or "Is … what you're saying?"

Most people don't use this strategy because they worry it makes it looks as if they agree with what was said. But validation is not about agreeing with someone. It's about showing they matter to you even though you disagree. Also, remember that you can't repeat what someone said if you're not actively listening. Therefore, make sure you're paying full attention to their words and body language.

2. Acknowledge the underlying emotion

In the previous chapter, we discussed how to acknowledge and respond to negative emotions. We all tend to avoid facing up to negative emotions in ourselves and others. We assume that if we suppress them, they'll just disappear, and the problem will simply go away. These days, it's all about "love and light" as people focus on feeling good all the time. It's like no one wants to face up to underlying dark emotions.

But these emotions never go away. They will pop up at some point and usually when you least expect them. In most cases, your negative emotions erupt when you're in an argument. To deal with conflict, you have to acknowledge the other person's underlying emotions. If someone seems sad or angry, you can't simply debate those emotions away. If you care about resolving the issue, you must care about their emotions. There are specific phrases you can use to validate someone's emotions. These include:

- *How did you feel when ...?*
- *That sounds scary/discouraging/frustrating.*
- *So you must have felt ..."*
- *On a scale of 1 to 10, how strong is that feeling?*

By asking such questions, you acknowledge the person's feelings and show them that it's OK to think or feel that way.

3. Accept their feelings and perspective

When you understand what someone is saying, you accept their thoughts and emotions. You're not saying you agree, but you accept that the person has them. Validation makes the person feel heard and affirmed.

Your words of validation make it clear you want to find common ground to resolve the issue. You can use statements such as "I understand why you feel the way you do," "Your feelings matter to me" or "I care about what you're saying." This is a more effective way to achieve mutual understanding than by arguing or debating with someone's feelings.

CHAPTER TAKEAWAYS

Conflict is a good way to pinpoint areas of friction in relationships so that you can resolve them. Here are six steps to help you resolve conflict:

- **Listen** – This is hard to do when the disagreement gets heated. But you need to allow the other person to vent their frustration about the issue. Let them share all their thoughts before you respond.
- **Practice mirroring** – You should mirror whatever you hear the other person say. Mirroring means repeating what the other person has said so they know you've heard them. For example, you can say "So what I hear you saying is that you find (a, b, c) very frustrating. Is that correct?" Mirroring diffuses

negative emotions and is an effective way to achieve a mutual understanding.

- **Ask questions** – You should ask the person for more information so they can get everything off their chest. For example, you can ask, "Is there anything else frustrating you about this issue?" If they add more thoughts, use mirroring to diffuse any frustrations.
- **Validate** – There are no right or wrong opinions. And there's no reason why you shouldn't validate the other person's feelings. Validating doesn't mean you agree with them. It means you care enough to see the situation from their perspective. You can say, "I understand why you feel that way. If I were in your shoes, I would probably feel that way about the situation."
- **Empathize** – You should understand what the other person is feeling so you can begin to resolve the conflict. For example, if your spouse is angry and feeling unappreciated, you can say, "I can see why you feel that nobody appreciates you despite all the work you do around here." If your spouse elaborates on this statement, then use mirroring, ask more questions and validate their feelings.
- **Respond** – The other person has shared all

their thoughts and feelings — now it's your turn. Use a positive tone of voice by staying calm and speaking in a kind and deliberate tone. Use positive body language by smiling, nodding your head often and maintaining eye contact. Pick your words carefully to avoid making the other person defensive. Don't speak in terms of absolutes by saying something like, "You *never* spend any time with me." Instead, speak in non-absolutes by saying, "*Sometimes* you don't spend enough time with me."

Once you've reached a mutual understanding with the other party, you're ready to move on to the next phase. Next, we'll learn about the third phase of conflict management—focusing on shared goals.

8

PHASE III – FOCUSING ON SHARED GOALS

We've discussed how to create mutual understanding by using empathy and validation. Once you' created mutual understanding, it is easier to find and agree on a win-win solution that serves the interests and needs of both parties. Each will have individual goals that are most likely opposed. Now it's time to identify any goals they have in common to start bringing everyone closer together.

But finding common ground is not as easy as it sounds. Keep your eyes on the target throughout the conflict resolution process and avoid distractions, especially petty personal issues that have little to do with the actual disagreement. If the conflict is intense, you need to build goodwill and create an environment conducive to resolution. Remember, your goal is to resolve the conflict while maintaining the relationship. However, you should also be prepared for an outcome that fails to preserve the relationship between the two parties.

Let's look at how to focus on common goals and create a sense of goodwill. We'll also consider how to save the relationship if both parties are unable to agree.

KEEPING YOUR EYES ON THE TARGET

As mentioned before, both sides in conflict have individual and shared needs. We have also talked about the importance of finding common ground to achieve a win-win situation. These are all great first steps focused on gathering information and solving problems. Consider these tools to help you deal with all kinds of conflict that may erupt in your personal or professional life.

And these tools are essential now more because we now live in a world of polarization. Whether it's in the workplace or at home, it seems like there's conflict everywhere. When a conflict arises, you have to find common ground. This can be very challenging for most people, which is why understanding conflict management skills is so valuable.

A report by Udemy, an online education company, revealed that conflict management is the most important soft skill required in the workplace. The report also stated that employees spend about three hours each week resolving conflicts. In other words, if you want to build and preserve trustworthy and dependable relationships, you must have conflict management skills.

Since conflict is inevitable, it's best to learn how to find common ground before it erupts. Be prepared to continually seek common ground during the entire conflict resolution process. This is how you'll stay focused on a win-win solution and building goodwill with the other party. There are several steps you can take to find common ground. Here are six ways to unlock an impasse:

Step 1: Assess your obstacles

The first question to ask when faced with conflict is, "What's standing in my way?" Think about any reasons the other party might have that would discourage them from reaching a compromise with you. Do they have a hidden agenda preventing you from finding common ground?

And asking yourself these questions can help determine the obstacles you might face in resolving the disagreement. Sometimes a person will disagree because they are fighting to maintain their values. In such cases, it's difficult to agree because the issue is tied to their identity. If so, you may need the intervention of a mediator or ground rules for engagement.

Step 2: Identify your top and bottom lines

Conflict resolution is a negotiation. It helps if you know your preferred outcome (top line), your alternatives and the point when you're willing to walk away (bottom line). As you contemplate how to get your way, also think about how to create something positive out of the negative situation.

Step 3: Select the right time and location

When seeking consensus with the other party in a conflict, focus on being calm and relaxed. Don't be upset or feel rushed because you have other things to do. If you're angry or irritated, take time to cool down before meeting with the other party. In terms of location, choose a neutral place such as a conference room or a coffee shop.

Step 4: Be curious

One of the biggest enemies of finding common ground is making assumptions. When you have preconceived notions, you won't ask questions or even hear anything the other person says. Instead, be curious about their values, beliefs and motivations. Put yourself in their shoes and listen as they express what they want. Ask them personal questions about family and hobbies to create a stronger connection. This will inspire them to open up and trust you, making it easier to reach a consensus.

Step 5: Identify the type of disagreement

There are three types of disagreements that lead to conflict. People tend to argue over individual values, basic facts or the best actions to take. Before you find common ground, you should know what type of disagreement you're dealing with. This means asking more questions and investigating the conflict's cause. For example, if you want to purchase cheaper raw materials to boost profit margins but your business partner believes the company should only provide high quality products, the conflict is based on values. But if your partner believes profit margins are OK and don't need to be increased, then that's a different disagreement altogether.

Step 6: Consult a third party

If finding common ground becomes too difficult, you should bring in a third party who can provide the necessary objectivity. They can defuse tension and pinpoint areas for agreement. A mediator can help prioritize issues, so you deal with the most pertinent things first. You'll learn more about using third parties later in this chapter.

HOW TO BUILD GOODWILL

Conflict tends to generate a lot of negativities such as anger, fear and disappointment. If you can turn that negativity into positive energy, you will build goodwill with the other person. Goodwill refers to a willing effort made to express positive concern for the other person. Let's say the other person in the conflict is angry and unwilling to put in the maximum effort to resolve the issue. You can decide to act the same and match their negativity or you can choose to put positive energy into the disagreement. And when you show goodwill by adding positivity, you yield greater results.

Goodwill is not a character trait that can be created out of thin air. It is a spontaneous emotional reflex that comes naturally from inside you. It's as simple as smiling and greeting your colleagues as you walk by them. It cannot be expressed by force.

But how do you express goodwill in a conflict situation? Here are some simple steps to build goodwill and trust with the other party:

1. **Take the first step** – Don't wait for the other

side to extend goodwill toward you. Be the first to greet them and ask questions to get to know their side of the story.
2. **Focus on the little things** – Goodwill is all about the little things. When you walk into a meeting, ask the other party how their day is going, speak kind words or crack a joke to make them laugh.
3. **Create mutual respect** – Both sides in the conflict must show respect if they want to find common ground. You will have different ideas and opinions but show the other side respect by supporting the process and appreciating their effort to seek a solution.
4. **Share constructive feedback** – Since you're already embroiled in a disagreement, offering negative feedback will only make things worse. Find a need or goal the other party has and offer constructive advice about it.
5. **Offer compliments** – Even if you disagree, you can still show appreciation to the other person for the work they do. Recognize any milestones they have achieved and show that you value their work or input.
6. **Practice what you preach** – When you say you're going to do something, stick to your word. Since conflict resolution is a negotiation,

the other person must see you as someone who follows through on promises.

7. **Be consistent** – Let your character be consistent regardless of where you go or who you are with. For example, don't pretend to be nice in the office and then be unpleasant out in public. Being two-faced destroys goodwill.
8. **Avoid gossip and complaining** – Don't criticize or be dismissive of the other person when talking to others. Gossip has a way of spreading and if they find out that you've been bad-mouthing them, they won't trust you.
9. **Don't use force** – You can't force the other party to accept your perspective. Bulldozing your way will only generate resentment and make resolving the conflict more difficult.

STRENGTHENING THE PARTNERSHIP

The conflict resolution process should be viewed more than a partnership than an adversarial contest. If you are a leader trying to bring two conflicting colleagues or teams together, then it's your job to find ways to bridge the gap between them. The two sides should see themselves as problem-solving partners and not opponents. Though we have talked through a lot of great tools so far, there is a four-stage model you can use to maintain and reinforce the partnership.

The first is the *Forming* stage. Both sides in the conflict are unsure of how they are going to overcome the disagreement. At this point your goal is to provide tasks that encourage team building so the two sides can get to know one another better.

The second is the *Storming* stage. This is when two people butt heads over their differences as they perform their tasks. As a leader, offer support throughout the conflict to help resolve it.

The third is the *Norming* stage. This is when the two people begin to identify similarities in each other, thus improving their interaction. Help them stay focused on the goal and encourage them to socially interact outside of work.

The final one is the *Performing* stage. Both people are now willing to work together. Continue to support them with resources and monitor their progress so they don't regress to a previous stage.

HOW TO PRESERVE THE RELATIONSHIP IN A HEATED CONFLICT

Heated conflicts tend to involve a lot of tension and emotions. As a result, you are likely to lose emotional control and say things that may harm the relationship in the long term. This is the biggest risk that comes with a heated conflict. When you fail to keep your emotions in check, you risk ruining valuable relationships.

Relationships are the basis of cooperation, collaboration and mutual understanding. And human beings are social creatures and rely on relationships—both personal and professional—to help navigate the highs and lows of life. Think about past times when you have experienced bad situations or unfortunate events in your life. I bet your family, friends or colleagues helped you get back on your feet. Your relationships are bridges and support systems that you can't afford to lose. This is why you want to work hard to preserve such bonds.

But preserving relationships during a conflict is not as easy as it may seem. When a conflict gets heated, the relationship is at stake. You want to control the situation to avoid long-term fallout. Here are four steps to preserve a relationship during a heated conflict:

Step 1: Focus on the bigger picture

When you're embroiled in an argument, you may feel you're being forced to give up a point of view, power or even respect. The conflict feels like a life-or-death situation, so your body prepares to fight or flee. But this shuts down the rational parts of your brain and leaves you emotionally charged. Thanks to mirror neurons, the other person sees the tension in your body and mimics your emotions. Before you know it, both of you have lost sight of the bigger picture and become focused on destroying each other.

To regain your focus, control your emotions. A simple way is to take deep breaths the moment you start feeling tense. You can also get up and walk around the room to help release the negative energy building up in your body. Just make sure you ask the other first, so you don't make them uncomfortable. You can also repeat a mantra in your head to stay calm, for example, "This isn't about me", or "This too shall pass."

Focusing on the bigger picture also involves searching for common ground. Look for areas you both agree on and work on achieving mutual understanding. Don't forget, this is a relationship that means a lot to you which is why you're taking the time to seek resolution. Though it's important to settle the issue, reaching an agreement is not the only priority. You both may still have to work together or live in the same house, so don't lose sight of preserving the relationship.

Step 2: Assume your counterpart has good intentions

When you're in a heated argument, it's easy to assume the other person is unreasonable and has bad intentions. But the truth is, that's rarely the case. Most conflicts are between two people who have good intentions but just hold different opinions. Pay attention and actively listen to what the other person says. Use the empathy and validation techniques we discussed in Chapter Six to show them you are present and listening with your heart. If you fail to listen or be empathetic, the other person will feel you aren't invested in the relationship or genuinely interested in resolving the conflict. This can damage your ability to resolve the issue.

Step 3: Use positive reframing

In a conflict, the words you use matter more than your intentions. You may want to calm a colleague down but how you speak will determine whether that happens or they get boiling mad. Learn how to choose the right words in an argument. Negative words are often used in a conflict because of the negative emotions involved. Improper assumptions can frame the conflict as a fight between right and wrong. Instead of finding the best way to resolve the issue, some people are quick to tell the other person how wrong they are. To make things worse, the other person may interpret words the wrong way. And then the hurt goes unnoticed because one speaker is too busy criticizing the other.

So how do you frame things positively and avoid escalating the conflict? A simple solution is to say nothing. You let the other person vent while you just listen. Once they've released their negative emotions, begin a productive conversation by asking questions such as, "Why did that make you angry?", or "What do you think about this situation?" This can help both parties get to the root cause of the argument. You can do your part by expressing your thoughts on the situation.

As you express yourself, frame your perspective using the right words. Here are some scenarios to help you find those words in a conflict situation.

Scenario #1: *As a manager, one of your team members is a hothead who is constantly arguing with others.*

You call the person into your office and say, "This team enjoys your input because you raise important issues that you feel strongly about. I know you want to have a good impact, so I want us to talk about whether you're achieving this goal in the team." This will make them contemplate the consequences of constant conflicts with teammates.

Scenario #2: *A co-worker angrily shouts at you because you said or did something.*

Stay silent and allow them to vent their frustration. Once they've calmed down, you can say, "It seems that what I said made you angry. I can't talk to you if you're yelling at me. How about we sit down and have a proper conversation to resolve this?"

Scenario #3: *You don't agree with your colleague or boss and want to offer some criticism.*

Focus on the underlying issue that you disagree on, whether it's a strategy, process or policy. And make sure you approach the person in private. You can say, "Michael, can I have a word with you? I want to understand the aim of this policy/strategy. Can you explain the rationale behind it? What will it accomplish?" After they answer your questions, you can offer alternatives that accomplish the same goal. You can say, "If that is the goal you want to accomplish, I have a different way to approach it. How about we …?"

Scenario #4: *You want to talk to your boss or colleague about a deadline you've missed or a mistake you've made.*

Get straight to the point and say, "I have some bad news to share. I should have said something sooner but here's the situation ..." Describe the problem and offer some solutions. You can say, "Those are some of my solutions to this situation. What do you think?" Be quick to take responsibility and don't try to rationalize why you made the mistake.

Step 4: Don't take things personally

When you disagree with someone, don't assume the other person dislikes you. The conflict is not about who you are. It's about what you may have said or done that hurt the person or interfered with their progress. It's easy to take things personally all the time, but look for where you're doing it so you can the habit. Here are some strategies to help you stop taking things personally:

- *Question your beliefs*

In most arguments, it is your interpretation of the situation that triggers your emotions and not the situation itself. When you greet someone and they don't respond, you feel disrespected and worthless. But why should you feel this way just because someone didn't say hello? It all comes down to your beliefs. You believe others should respond to your greeting. If they don't, they must think you're worthless. Question this belief and consider that returning a greeting is not about you—it's about them. Maybe they didn't hear you or are having a bad day. Start questioning your beliefs when you feel offended by someone's behavior.

- *Don't worry about others' opinions*

Why do you care so much what people think about you? Most of us have been brainwashed from childhood into believing everyone should like and accept us. The truth is that you can't control whether others approve of you. You can say or do everything right but whether others like you is up to them. Just accept yourself as you are, act in the best way possible and don't worry about what people think.

- *Be aware of the "spotlight effect"*

The "spotlight effect" is the tendency to think there's a spotlight on you and everyone sees your flaws. We all do it — overestimate our weaknesses and assume people are pointing them out. But in most cases, this is only happening in our minds. For example, you may feel a colleague is criticizing your work when in reality they aren't even referring to you at all. Be aware of this tendency so you can avoid taking things personally.

- *Ignore trolls and delete their comments*

In a world where social media consumes so much of our time and attention, someone is inevitably going to comment about you. Some can be extremely insulting. If you take things personally, you may find yourself embroiled in a Twitter brawl with someone you'll never meet. Recognize trolls when you see them online. Simply delete their comments from your social media page and move on with your life.

WHAT IF YOU CAN'T SALVAGE THE RELATIONSHIP?

There will be times when your attempts to solve a conflict fail and reconciliation becomes difficult. If the situation becomes untenable, then it's time to step back and think about what you can do. If the two sides can't reach a solution, consider involving a mediator to help find common ground and shared interests. At the same time, understand that some conflicts can't be resolved in the first attempt. You must be willing to walk away and take time to clear your mind.

As you take a break from the conflict, sit back and reflect on the conversations that occurred during the process. Think about what both sides said and what you learned from their exchanges. And don't forget, some conflicts just won't end in a win-win situation. If collaboration or accommodating has failed, you may need to adopt a compromising style of conflict resolution.

If you can't compromise at all, maybe the bond you share is beyond saving. Think about this option and prepare yourself emotionally so you're ready to tell the other party your decision. Be prepared to forgive and forget the negative things that may have been said or done. The other person may be contemplating a similar decision so be willing to accept their apology. Don't hold grudges and be prepared to move forward with your life.

Although moving on may be difficult, accept that you tried your best. Don't judge yourself or the other person too harshly and avoid focusing on the negative aspects of the relationship. This will only prevent you from moving forward. Be empathetic toward all involved and agree to part ways amicably.

CHAPTER TAKEAWAYS

Taking things personally is one of the biggest reasons why we get into arguments and create conflict situations in relationships. So here are some more insights on why you shouldn't take things personally:

- When others insult or lie to you directly, understand it has nothing to do with you. Their opinion is a reflection of who they are and their mental and emotional state.
- You become prey when you take things personally. The other person can manipulate you, causing you to suffer for nothing.
- By learning not to take things personally, you achieve personal freedom and live life on your terms.
- If you take things personally, the other person can feed you emotional poison and you'll eat it up.
- By refusing to take this emotional poison, you become immune, and the sender is the one who suffers.

Learning to manage conflict is like learning magic. You must explore its fundamental aspects to become a master of the craft. Next, let's discuss how to get to the root of conflict as you find possible solutions to the problem.

9

PHASE IV – THE ROOT OF CONFLICT

Every conflict has an underlying cause. It's not always easy to find this root cause because it's often buried beneath raw emotions and words thrown around in the argument. Most people are quick to jump straight into the conflict to treat the symptoms without considering the deeper problem that needs to be resolved. But as a result, you might end up stopping the argument on the surface, but the conflict will most certainly reappear later.

And when that happens, you're likely to get frustrated because you thought you'd solved the problem permanently. You may find yourself fixing the same issue repeatedly with each episode worse than the previous one. Let's look at how to strip away the layers of illusion to reveal the truth beneath the façade.

But how do you uncover this truth so you can resolve the conflict permanently? You have to dig deeper to uncover the root cause. This is the only way to find and resolve the problem's source rather than the symptoms on the surface. Let's look at how to find the root cause of a conflict by using root cause analysis. We'll also identify tools and techniques to identify possible solutions to the problem.

TRACING THE ORIGINS

One of the most popular techniques used to trace a problem's origin is root cause analysis (RCA). This involves using a series of steps and tools to identify the source of a problem. The RCA method helps you determine what happened, why it happened and how to prevent it from happening again. One of the assumptions that RCA makes is that systems and events are connected. An action that occurs in one area triggers an action in a different area and so on. When you trace these actions backward, you can identify the cause of the problem and how it escalated into the symptoms you're seeing.

Using the RCA technique, you're likely to identify three causes of problems:

- **Physical causes** – These are material or

tangible things that failed to work properly. For example, your manager is angry at you for failing to send a report on time. The real cause is that the server crashed, and the information technology (IT) technician couldn't fix it in time.

- **Human causes** – Someone made a mistake or failed to take action when necessary. For example, the IT department failed to debug the system on schedule.
- **Organizational causes** – The organization's systems or policies don't work as they should. For example, system maintenance is supposed to be handled by a team and everyone on it assumes someone else has already debugged the system.

You can use RCA to identify the cause of a problem in any situation. You should be able to explore the pattern of events and specific actions that led to the conflict. However, don't be surprised if you find multiple root causes. If so, make sure you focus on the most significant and resolvable causes. To identify the problem's most significant root cause(s), you need to follow a specific process. The RCA process involves five key steps, including:

Step 1: Define the problem

The first thing to do when a conflict breaks out is define the problem. Look at the situation to determine what is happening on the surface. For example, what is each person saying? How are they reacting to each other? Your aim here is to identify the specific symptoms of the problem.

Step 2: Gather data

Once you've identified the symptoms, start gathering data so you can fully analyze the situation. Look for tangible proof the problem exists and identify its impact on the people involved as well as those around them. You should also search for data that shows how long the problem has existed. The best way to do this is by talking to everyone who understands the conflict. For example, if two students are engaged in a conflict, you should talk to them, their friends, classmates and even teachers. The more familiar someone is with the argument, the more valuable their information is.

Step 3: Pinpoint possible causal factors

In this step, you need to identify the series of events that led to the conflict. Specific conditions allowed the situation to occur. You should pinpoint these conditions and any other problems influencing the conflict. Your goal is to find as many causal factors as possible.

For example, the two students may be arguing over a project they were supposed to complete together. However, the conflict could also be caused by cultural differences or one of them feeling disrespected by the other.

Dig deeper to uncover seemingly small issues that may be playing a role in the conflict. Four tools that can help you pinpoint these causal factors include:

- **Appreciation** – You ask a series of "So what?" questions to identify the potential consequences of a fact.
- **Five whys** – You ask a series of five "Why?" questions until you find the situation's root cause.
- **Drill down** – You dissect the problem into smaller parts to home in on the finer details.
- **Cause-and-effect diagrams** – You make a chart that shows all the potential causal factors.

These tools are discussed in greater detail in the next section of this chapter.

Step 4: Find the root cause

Once you've uncovered as many causal factors as possible, identify why they exist. You can use the tools outlined in Step 3 above to dig deeper and find the underlying reason for the problem.

Step 5: Recommend and implement solutions

At this stage, you should be looking for ways to prevent the conflict from happening again. Figure out how the solution will be implemented and who will be in charge of implementation. You should also consider any risks that may arise from the solution. This allows you to pinpoint any potential failure factors.

One tool you can use to spot any potential weaknesses of the solution is failure mode and effects analysis (FMEA). This risk analysis tool identifies areas where your solution may fail. You can also use impact analysis as a tool to minimize the negative consequences of the solution.

TOOLS FOR IDENTIFYING POTENTIAL CAUSAL FACTORS

As mentioned in the previous section, identifying the possible causal factors of a conflict is the third step in RCA. Once you've defined the problem and gathered enough data for analysis, next determine all the factors that may have triggered the conflict. Usually when a conflict breaks out, it's difficult to perceive the real cause of the problem. Even if you quickly identify a specific cause, there are likely to be other underlying conditions and factors influencing the conflict.

Your goal should be to uncover as many of these underlying causal factors as you can. This is possible by using the four tools described below. They can help you better understand the problem and get to its root as quickly as possible. These tools help you break down what seems like a major problem into manageable parts so you can identify all possible causes.

Keep in mind that no one tool can solve every kind of problem. Each has its pros and cons. Sometimes you have to combine different techniques to find a more effective solution. Here are four tools you can use to pinpoint the conflict's causal factors:

Appreciation

This is a technique developed by the military to help you extract as much information as possible from a simple statement. It allows you to uncover factors that are not easily discernible so you can gain a broad understanding of any situation. You start with a factual statement and then ask a series of "So what?" questions. Keep asking the same question until you have drawn as many conclusions as possible. Here is an example of how to use this tool.

Your organization just announced your department's budget will be reduced by 20%. As the manager, you want to know all of the potential consequences, so you formulate a statement and ask "So what?" questions:

Statement: The budget is being slashed by 20%.

- So what?

So we now have to cut spending to accommodate the reduced budget.

- So what?

So we may have to lay off staff, freeze hiring new talent and cut supply spending.

- So what?

So I have to find cheaper sources of supplies and more ways of boosting team morale.

- So what?

So, I need to prepare my team for the changes that will arise from this new budget.

One thing to note about the appreciation technique is that it can limit you to a single line of thought. The answer to the first "So what?" question may lead you down a single path of inquiry instead of expanding your options. So, think about repeating the entire process multiple times to cover all your bases.

Five whys

This technique was developed by the Japanese inventor and industrialist Sakichi Toyoda. It involves cutting through the external symptoms of a problem to identify its underlying causes. Here, your goal is to create countermeasures rather than solutions. Countermeasures are actions that prevent a problem from recurring whereas a solution makes the symptoms go away.

This technique is useful when troubleshooting or resolving problems that are simple or moderately challenging. It isn't as effective when handling complex issues because it may lead you down a single path of inquiry. In situations where there may be multiple causal factors, you're better off using a broader-based tool such as the cause-and-effect diagram.

But the "Five Whys" technique is still useful due to its simplicity and ability to quickly uncover the root cause of a conflict. It also offers flexibility and can easily be combined with other RCA tools. When you're facing a conflict between two people, use the "Five Whys" before attempting another in-depth technique.

The "Five Whys" process has seven steps:

Step 1: Gather your team

Assemble the people who understand the conflict's intricate details. Pick someone to be a facilitator during the process. Their job is to keep everyone focused on finding the best countermeasures.

Step 2: State the problem

Discuss the conflict with your team and, if possible, observe the conflict as it takes place. Get the team to agree on a brief, yet clear problem statement. For example, "A client refuses to pay for the brochures we printed." Write this statement on a whiteboard or piece of paper with enough space around the statement for answers.

Step 3: Ask "Why?"

Ask the first "Why?" question. For example, "Why has the client refused to pay for the brochures we printed?" Let the team provide possible, yet credible answers based on fact rather than guesses. Write down the answer(s) as brief phrases beside the problem statement. For example, "We didn't deliver the brochures to the client on time so they couldn't use them when she needed to."

The question sounds simple, but it calls for serious thought as the team must provide accounts of actual events. Relying on deductive reasoning can lead to a huge number of causal factors that have little to do with the problem at hand.

Step 4: Ask four more "Whys?"

After generating the first answer, ask four more "Why?" questions. Frame each question according to the previous response. For example:

"Why were the brochures delivered late?"

"It took longer than expected to complete the task."

"Why did it take longer than expected to complete the task?"

"We ran out of printer ink."

Why did we run out of printer ink?"

"We used all the ink on a large printing order that came in at the last minute."

"Why did we use all the ink on this last-minute order?"

"There wasn't enough ink in stock and not enough time to order more."

And this allows you to find the countermeasure — to search for a supplier who can deliver ink at short notice to allow the organization to quickly respond to increased customer demand.

Step 5: Know when it's time to stop

When the questions no longer provide you with useful responses, you'll know it's time to stop. The last countermeasure that you've written down should be the most appropriate action to take. If you feel you need to explore further for a deeper root cause, you can use the cause-and-effect diagram. If necessary, keep going and ask more than five "Whys?" to find the root cause. In other situations, it may only take three or four questions to uncover the problem's underlying cause.

Step 6: Resolve the root cause

Once you've found the root cause(s), have your team discuss and agree on the countermeasures. Develop a plan on how to implement each countermeasure to prevent the conflict from recurring.

Step 7: Track your countermeasures

Pay attention to how effectively your countermeasures resolved the conflict. If necessary, amend or replace any countermeasure that isn't working. And if countermeasures aren't as effective as you thought they would be, you can repeat the whole process to identify the right root cause(s).

Drill down

This is a simple technique that involves breaking down complex problems into components until you solve the problem. Your goal is to break the problem into smaller, more manageable causes. You then take each cause and break it down progressively until you have a comprehensive understanding of the whole problem. These smaller causes are then used as the basis for a solution. If you get stuck in breaking down a particular point using the knowledge you have, do some research or talk to an expert.

In the drill-down method, you write down the main problem in the left column of a large sheet of paper. You then hold a brainstorming session where you elaborate on any related issues in the right column. This could be any information related to the problem or factors affecting it. You can even include questions about the main problem. Here are the four steps used in the drill-down technique:

1. Write down the main problem

First take an inventory of the main problem. Be specific when describing it. For example, write down the names of the people involved in and affected by the conflict. Ensure everyone who is connected to the conflict participates in the brainstorming session as they can provide deeper insight into the problem. Focus on describing the main conflict and avoid engaging in trivial problems or considering unrealistic expectations.

2. Identify the causes of the conflict

In this step, determine the underlying factors causing the conflict. These likely include individuals and situations that contributed to the conflict. An effective way to find the underlying causes is to incorporate the "Five Whys" technique while performing the drill down. After you've stated the main problem, ask a series of "Why?" questions to identify the underlying causes. At the end of this step, take a break before coming back to develop a plan.

3. Develop a plan

Once you've identified the conflict's root causes, develop a plan that resolves the problem. It should be detailed, clear and specific. Identify and write down every task that needs to be done and who will be responsible for them. Establish a timeline for implementing the plan and include strategies for measuring the results. The implementation plan should also account for any risks or challenges that may arise. And make sure both sides in the conflict agree to the plans to ensure smooth implementation.

4. Put the plan into action

The final step is to execute the implementation plan and document the progress of the measures put in place. If the plan is effective, the conflict won't arise again. If it reappears, consider whether you identified all the underlying causes. You may need to repeat the process to uncover causes you may have missed or ignored.

Cause-and-effect diagrams

The cause-and-effect diagram is effective in exploring the root causes of serious problems. It is also known as a fishbone or Ishikawa diagram. Unlike the tools mentioned above, this one lets you dig deeper to uncover all the conflict's possible causes instead of the most obvious ones. You can also use it to uncover bottlenecks in a conflict resolution process. There are four steps used in a cause-and-effect diagram:

1. Identify the problem

Draw a box on the left side of a large sheet of paper and write the main problem in it. Let's say the problem is an unproductive team member named Mike. After you've written down the problem inside the box, draw a horizontal line stretching from the box all across the paper. This is the "spine" of the diagram.

2. Identify the major factors

Identify all the factors that are part of the problem. These factors could be the involved parties, materials, equipment, systems or even other people. You can brainstorm with others to identify as many factors as possible that affect the conflict. Let's say the factors that affect Mike's lack of cooperation are the task, equipment and fellow team members. Draw a diagonal line off the "spine" for every factor you've identified. Each of these smaller lines, or "bones," should be labeled according to the factor identified. Here you would d end up with three lines labeled, "Task," "Equipment" and "Team members."

3. Determine possible causes

Identify the possible causes of every factor identified in Step 2. Draw a shorter line off the "bone" lines to represent each cause. If a possible cause is too complex, split it into sub-causes. Each sub-cause will be a separate line coming off the main cause line. For example, after a brainstorming session, you discover two team members, Jane and John, are possible causes for Mike's unproductivity. Draw two lines off the "Team members" line and label them "Jane" and "John." Keep breaking down each cause and sub-cause until you can't find any more possible causes.

4. Analyze the diagram

Now your diagram should have enough possible causes for you to investigate. If the conflict is complex, start by investigating the most likely causes. You can use surveys or face-to-face interviews to identify which potential cause is truly triggering the conflict.

Finding the conflict's root cause can help both sides focus their energies on eliminating it while preserving the relationship. It's important all parties in the conflict agree on the root cause. It is only when both sides are in consensus that it's possible to find and implement an effective solution to the problem. So be sure to use the ground rules we talked about in Chapter Five when seeking solutions to the conflict. An especially important rule is to withhold judgment and embrace all ideas when brainstorming for potential solutions.

During the brainstorming process, analyze all potential ideas and eliminate all solutions that aren't mutually beneficial. Highlight and encourage win-win solutions that result in a better outcome for both parties. It's better to generate as many ideas as possible so you have multiple options in case a particular solution fails. And you can be creative and combine various ideas to improve the chances of minimizing loss and maximizing a favorable outcome. The best way to decrease damage and increase benefits is to continually analyze and evaluate ideas based on how mutually beneficial they are.

CHAPTER TAKEAWAYS

Conflict is often triggered by perceptions that don't accurately reflect the intentions of the other person. That's why you should ask questions at various stages of the conflict resolution process. Questions help create empathy and trust. They also help you understand perceptions and agree on possible solutions. Here are some questions to ask the other person in the conflict:

- *How did that make you feel?*
- *Can you tell me why you feel angry?*
- *Are you frustrated because ...?*
- *What steps can we take to build trust between us?*
- *What can I do to show you that I'm worthy of your trust?*
- *What does trust mean to you?*
- *What were your intentions when you said...?*
- *How did you perceive my words/behavior?*
- *May I explain what I intended when I did/said...?*
- *How will this conflict affect our relationship moving forward?*
- *What can we do to repair the harm this conflict has brought to our relationship?*
- *Do you see a future between us?*
- *What are you willing to let go of to resolve this conflict?*

You can also ask yourself the following questions:

- *How is this conflict helping me?*
- *How is it affecting my health and relationships?*
- *What emotions am I feeling due to this conflict?*
- *What has this conflict revealed about my values?*
- *What happens if I just let it go?*
- *What am I willing to let go to resolve it?*
- *What am I not willing to accept?*

- *What would an acceptable resolution look like?*
- *How will resolving this conflict serve my interests?*
- *Do I need to distance myself from this person?*

This chapter has covered the first part of Phase IV of conflict management, how to find the conflict's root cause. Keep in mind that in this phase, you should brainstorm ideas continuously until you identify and successfully implement a solution. Next, we'll keep learning about this phase and look at how to facilitate the various solutions you've generated.

10

PHASE IV – TAKING ACTION

We've looked at processes to find a conflict's root cause. And we've discovered how to use various tools and techniques to uncover the cause of a problem. Once you have found the cause and are satisfied you have gotten to the bottom of the disagreement, the next step is to take the necessary action to resolve the conflict.

Resolving a conflict is a process that involves finding a solution that satisfies all the parties involved. Each person has their own interests and will use their power to ensure their goals are met. The negotiation process can sometimes get messy due to a variety of elements. One person may hold ideas and opinions that are contrary to the other. Raw emotions may hinder the negotiation's progress. And personality clashes, communication styles and even time pressures are also elements that can affect a negotiation.

Despite all elements that threaten to derail the process, both sides must work together to find an optimal and mutually acceptable solution. They must be willing to communicate and compromise. Let's turn now to understanding the art of negotiation, the various steps and stages of the process and the factors that can help you create a win-win solution.

THE PATH OF NEGOTIATION

Negotiation refers to the back-and-forth communication between you and another party to reach an agreement where both sides have mutual as well as contrary interests. It is a process of settling differences by reaching an agreement while avoiding arguments.

In every disagreement, each side aims to achieve an outcome that best suits their position. The disagreement may be within an organization, between two governments or in a domestic relationship. Whatever the situation, the principles of mutual benefit, fairness and relationships must be applied to ensure a successful negotiation.

The specific form of negotiation will depend on the situation. Some may require a higher level of negotiating skills than others. Negotiating a trade dispute between two countries requires a different set of skills than resolving an argument between your teenage children. But whatever situation you're in, you at least need some general negotiation skills that can be applied to a wide range of circumstances. These skills can help you achieve a desirable outcome when disputes arise between you and others.

Achieving a desirable outcome in a negotiation requires that you follow a structured methodology. Negotiation is a process, and every process must go through a specific set of steps to achieve its goals. When negotiating a conflict, there are six stages, including:

Stage 1: Preparation

Before any negotiation takes place, both sides must agree on when and where they should meet. They should also decide who will attend the meeting and its timeframe. In this first stage, all the relevant facts of the disagreement should be put on the table to clarify everyone's position.

For example, if it's a family dispute, decide whether the disagreement should be resolved internally or require a counselor. If it's a workplace dispute, refer to the organization's rules and policies to guide your approach.

Stage 2: Discussion

This is the stage when both sides present their case according to their view of the situation. Some skills are critical during this stage such as listening, questioning and clarifying. As we've talked about before, listening is very important because most people tend to talk more than they listen during a disagreement. Both sides must be given equal opportunity to argue their case. Depending on the situation, you may need to take notes to record all the argument points. This information can be used later in case further clarification is needed.

Stage 3: Clarification of goals

As the discussion continues, both sides should clarify their goals, viewpoints and interests. Prioritize your list of goals as this can help identify common ground with the other person. By clarifying your goals, you minimize the chances of misunderstandings down the road. Such misunderstandings have the potential of derailing a mutually beneficial outcome.

Stage 4: Finding a win-win outcome

In this stage, focus on finding an outcome where both sides gain something positive from the negotiation. Both people need to feel their viewpoint has been factored into the negotiation's outcome. Though a win-win outcome is always the goal, sometimes it may be impossible to achieve. And when this occurs, you need to suggest alternative solutions that may involve compromises by both sides.

Stage 5: Agreement

Once both sides have considered and now understand each other's interests and viewpoints, an agreement can be reached. Don't forget, though, that everyone will need to stay open-minded to reach a mutually acceptable solution. The agreement must be clear, so everyone understands the decision being made.

Stage 6: Implementation

Lastly, take a course of action that ensures the solution is implemented. Both sides must commit to implementing the plan as agreed upon. This means there should be a sense of accountability from both parties as well as a monitoring of results to prevent a recurrence of the conflict.

RATIONAL AND EMOTIONAL ELEMENTS OF NEGOTIATION

There are two decision-making processes you go through during every negotiation. There is the rational (substantive) process and then there's the emotional (psychological) process. Both play key roles in determining the outcome of a negotiation. By far, the main element that leads to negotiation failure is the emotional process. But why do emotional factors negatively affect negotiations in such a major way?

The truth is that it's easier to understand the rational element of a negotiation than the emotional part. To understand the rational part, you just have to examine the facts laid out on the table. However, most people don't have a strong understanding of their psychological makeup, much less that of the other party in a conflict. And this inability to understand the emotional issues and needs is what causes most negotiations to fail.

The failure of two parties to agree on an optimal solution during a negotiation usually arises from several factors such as:

- How comfortable each individual feels about conflict
- How much one side hates or likes the other
- The perception each side has about the other
- The assumptions each side makes about the problem
- The expectations and attitudes about the other side
- How important trust is to each side

- The importance each side attaches to "winning" and not looking bad in front of the other side

And this lack of emotional understanding is usually worse within organizations. Few businesses encourage their employees to openly express negative emotions. As a result, many employees are forced to express their intense emotional conflicts under the guise of a rational argument. An employee will stir up a dispute with their colleague over a trivial issue to justify an emotional conflict they have with that person. For example, you start an argument over some grammatical errors in a report. However, your real problem is that you felt disrespected during the last team meeting. Since you can't express your anger openly, you look for a rational excuse to rage at your colleague. This kind of conflict is more difficult to resolve because of its hidden underlying factors.

If these factors are not exposed, the negotiation process will break down and both sides may fail to agree. If this happens, the best step is to reschedule or call for another meeting. When a negotiation breaks down, a heated argument often erupts as both parties get bogged down in useless drama and chest-thumping. By scheduling another meeting, you avoid wasting time and potentially damaging the relationship.

During this next meeting, you should repeat Stages 1 to 6 of the negotiation process. This time, look for new ideas and examine the situation from a different perspective. Consider other alternative solutions and, if necessary, ask for a mediator's help.

DISTRIBUTIVE VS. INTEGRATIVE NEGOTIATIONS

Every bargaining situation can be classified into two major categories: distributive or integrative. Distributive negotiations are also known as win-lose or zero-sum negotiations. This is the same as the competitive conflict management style we talked about in Chapter Three. One side must win and the other must lose. This kind of bargaining is used in situations where resources are fixed and must be shared. For example, when buying a car, the more the seller gets of your money, the less you have left. If the other side must lose for you to win, both sides will be solely focused on maximizing their interests. This usually leads to underhanded tactics such as force, manipulation and hiding relevant information. The goal is to "claim value" so you reduce the other person's value as you raise your own.

Integrative negotiation is a win-win or collaborative type of bargaining. And here, both sides get what they want because available resources aren't fixed. Both focus on achieving a mutually acceptable outcome. For example, you and your spouse cannot agree on where to go for a dinner date. Another example is resolving a conflict with a subordinate who constantly shows up late for work.

In such situations, it's possible to negotiate and end up with a win-win outcome. The tactics include cooperation, mutual problem-solving and shared information. The goal here is to "create value" so both sides end up feeling they have more value than before the negotiation.

This kind of win-win negotiation should be your primary focus. Both sides must collaborate if you want to end up with an integrative negotiation rather than a distributive one.

Here are some critical points to help you conduct an integrative negotiation:

Plan for the negotiation

Before negotiation begins, determine whether you are in a collaborative or competitive situation. This will help you know what kind of approach to take to achieve your objectives. You also need to clarify underlying interests and goals. Be very clear about what is important to you and find out what the other side expects from the negotiation. This can help you craft a suitable strategy.

As you contemplate your strategy, think about what the best resolution would look like for both parties. Would such a resolution be fair and reasonable to both sides? You need to think about these issues before negotiation so you know what a successful outcome would look like. Too many people waste so much time worrying about the other side winning that they forget their own needs and goals. Focus on getting your ideal outcome — not blocking the other side from achieving their goal.

Create a min-max strategy

When entering a negotiation, you're already thinking about how to maximize the situation to achieve your goals. But don't forget to figure out what a minimally acceptable deal looks like. Think about the circumstances that would force you to walk away from the negotiation. Here are some questions to ask yourself when planning your min-max strategy:

1. *What are the minimum conditions I can accept in this negotiation?*
2. *What is the minimum I can offer the other side without offending them?*

3. What are the maximum conditions I can ask for without offending them?
4. What is the maximum I can offer them?

As you contemplate these issues, you should think about how the other side would answer the same questions. These questions will help you determine your strongest and weakest points as well as the advantages and disadvantages of the other side's argument.

Separate the personality from the problem

Avoid attacking the other person's personality and instead focus on addressing the problem. When one side feels threatened, they automatically become defensive and begin to counterattack their opponent. This leads to an emotional debate that can steer the negotiation away from critical underlying issues. Instead, stay rational and focus on your goals even if the other person attacks you personally. Let them vent their frustration but don't allow yourself to get sucked into an emotional reaction. Use the techniques we talked about in Chapter Seven to help you not take things personally. Remember–don't drink the poison!

Emphasize win-win solutions

It is possible to create a win-win solution from what seems to be a win-lose situation. For example, you can make low-cost concessions that are of great value to the other party. You can also reframe a solution to reflect their interests. Focus on creating an integrative solution that allows both sides to walk away feeling victorious.

Find underlying interests

When negotiating to resolve a conflict, seek to understand the other side's underlying interests and needs. Ask questions and exchange information to find common ground. Because when you understand the other side's interests, sometimes you realize they are similar to your own. This is what leads to integrative bargaining where both sides are focused on creating a win-win situation.

Use an objective standard

Negotiations require a high level of objectivity. In other words, let the outcome be based on objective criteria that both sides agree on. This is a better approach than allowing your subjective emotions to take over.

Empathize with the other side

There is always more than one side to a conflict. It's not just about you and what you want. Therefore, resolving conflict means empathizing with the other side's goals and needs. Think about their personality and how far you can push during negotiations. If you use too much aggression or deception, you may push them to the point they worry they are going to lose the negotiation. This can create resentment and retaliation. Even if they let you win, they won't be committed to the solution. The only way to ensure they stay true to the solution is to consider their wants and needs. Think about how you can reframe potential solutions to fit their interests.

Know your BATNA

BATNA stands for "Best Alternative to a Negotiated Agreement." It is your most preferred alternative if the other party doesn't agree with your primary goal. You can find your BATNA by exploring a range of attractive options. Evaluate them and choose the one that seems most promising. And don't forget to find out the other person's BATNA and try to change it so it aligns with your goals. If you notice that their BATNA is weak, it means they don't have much room to maneuver, leaving you in a better position.

Practice active listening

Active listening was covered extensively in Chapter Five, so you already know that it's a key component of conflict resolution. To be an active listener, pay attention to what the other person is saying verbally and nonverbally. You should continuously check that you understand what they are saying. Ask clarifying questions or restate the other person's comments to ensure you heard them correctly. And focus on talking about solutions rather than blaming the other side for the conflict. Active listening shows the other side you are genuine in wanting to find a win-win solution.

CREATING AN OPTIMAL SOLUTION

As you work toward finding an optimal conflict resolution, think about the criteria you will use to help you evaluate all the solutions you've come up with. These should enable you to find a feasible and profitable solution that aligns with a win-win scenario. It should also ensure there are minimal compromises for both sides. There are several factors you should consider when evaluating available solutions, including:

- The aims of each solution
- The individual wants and needs that the solution fulfills
- The shared goals that the solution fulfills
- The compromises that each side must accept

A careful evaluation of each potential solution using these criteria will help you create a plan that will effectively resolve the conflict. This plan should incorporate all the elements discussed during the negotiation. And it should follow a particular structure so the plan is as comprehensive as possible. To ensure the plan has a well-developed structure, you need to ask the following questions:

- *How will the solution be implemented?*
- *What efforts must each party make to ensure the plan is successful?*
- *Are both sides willing to make these efforts?*
- *What does the result look like?*
- *Do both parties agree to this result?*
- *What steps should be implemented first?*
- *What are the requirements that must be fulfilled?*

Once the plan is ready, act on it right away. During the implementation, it's important to stick to the ground rules discussed in Chapter Six. For example, you need periodic meetings to check the plan's progress. If the conflict was a personal one, don't shy away from asking your family, friend or partner how things are going on their end. Ask them if they need help with anything to ensure the plan stays on track.

Discuss the solution being implemented to determine if the original plan needs any adjustments. Keep evaluating all the relevant factors and holding regular meetings until the problem is resolved and the conflict is eliminated.

CHAPTER TAKEAWAYS

You find yourself negotiating with someone who isn't interested in achieving a win-win solution. No matter what you do, the conflict keeps escalating and it seems you're heading for a win-lose situation. What do you do? How do you turn a win-lose into a win-win situation? Here are several techniques to use:

- If the other party is venting, acknowledge their frustrations and listen to what they say. If possible, use humor to reduce tension in the room or consider making a small concession as a sign of good faith.
- Find ways to establish commonalities by identifying a mutual enemy. The enemy should be a situation rather than a person. This will minimize your perceived differences and encourage the other side to change their perspective of you.
- Find a way to split the conflict into smaller issues. It may be easier to find common ground on several small issues than one large issue. You may end up with several smaller win-win

solutions although you concede ground in others.
- If the other side makes an unreasonable offer, identify ways of repackaging their demand to make it more aligned with your goals. Find ways to sweeten their offer and refine their proposal so you don't end up losing completely.
- Place greater emphasis on understanding the needs of the other person. Focus more on moving toward their position and less on your own. You can do this gradually in the hope they will take a similar approach.

We've now discovered the four stages of conflict resolution. Next, we will look at specific suggestions on how to facilitate conflict resolution in your personal and professional relationships.

11

FACILITATING PERSONAL AND PROFESSIONAL CONFLICT RESOLUTION

So far we've discussed conflict resolution from a general perspective. We've covered a range of tools and techniques to help you manage any conflict that arises. But there's also a need to identify specific tools and strategies optimized for specific situations. Though the techniques we covered in previous chapters will work in any conflict situation, sometimes you need to use a strategy that fits the conflict's particular context.

For example, a conflict between you and your spouse has a very different connotation than one between you and a colleague. Although you can use a similar approach in both cases, consider the subtle nuances that are involved in each situation. You and your spouse are intimate partners who live together, and these factors will influence how you go about resolving conflict. On the other hand, a conflict with a colleague isn't necessarily an intimate one but it has the potential of costing you a source of income or career.

In a conflict, keep in mind the undertones that define the relationship you have with the other person. Next, we'll offer suggestions on how to facilitate conflict resolution with your spouse as well as how to teach your children to handle conflict. We'll also look at how to maintain a conflict-free workplace, especially concerning generational and cultural conflicts.

RESOLVING MARITAL CONFLICTS

Most of the approaches we discussed in the previous chapters will help you handle all kinds of conflicts. But when it comes to marital conflicts, there are a few extra things you need to consider. Resolving a conflict with your spouse in a peaceful manner is not easy. This is especially true during the early months and years of your marriage. Two individuals with unique personalities and backgrounds now live together, creating a recipe for all kinds of disagreements. There will be arguments over taking out the garbage, whether the toilet seat should be up or down, what to do with the spare bedroom and which TV show to watch.

Such disagreements may seem minor but they can have a great bearing on your marriage. As we mentioned in Chapter One, conflict is inevitable and marital conflict can easily trigger a negative spiral of emotion that gradually damages the relationship. And if left unresolved, the conflict can result in communication problems, anger, resentment, feelings of revenge and ultimately divorce.

These are dire consequences for a couple who expected to stay together forever. For this reason, you want to avoid engaging in constant conflict with your spouse. When conflicts become the norm rather than the exception, you are likely to experience arguments, fights and unhappiness in your marriage. This creates distance between you and your spouse. And it becomes difficult to reconcile without first tackling the underlying causes of the conflict.

Causes of conflict in marriage

Resolving marital conflict is not easy. Put yourself in your spouse's shoes, listen to what they say and keep an open mind. There should be healthy debate as both sides take turns speaking about the conflict. If it's a straightforward issue, you can reach some sort of compromise.

But sometimes the issue that triggered the conflict is a major one and reaching a compromise is difficult. In that case, you both need to take a break and revisit the issue over several days. The most important thing is to be respectful and loving. Maintaining an open mind and staying true to yourself can go a long way in helping you prevent and resolve conflicts in your relationship.

Respect, love and open-mindedness can help you uncover the root cause of the conflict. You must find these causes and address them before they do further damage to your marriage. Some of these root causes include:

- Criticism
- Sarcasm
- Spending of money
- Lack of trust
- When to have or how to raise children
- Quick temperament
- Name-calling
- Past unresolved conflicts
- Lack of effective communication
- Different marital expectations
- Extramarital affairs
- Not enough sex or too much of it

Examine your relationship and communicate with your partner to find the underlying causes of your conflict. Be willing to dig deep into every issue and avoid the urge to become defensive when you're called out by your partner. Once you've unearthed these root causes, you'll be ready to resolve the conflict.

HOW TO RESOLVE A MARITAL CONFLICT

We live in a time where reality shows and dating apps make relationships seem easy. Modern culture has created a façade where most people believe all they need to do is swipe right on their smartphone and voila! A relationship manifests and you live happily ever after. But maintaining a romantic relationship takes work and when you don't invest the required time and energy, things can get tough. This is when disagreements break out and you're forced to deal with conflict.

A marital conflict can flare up for several reasons. Some are minor such as who takes the garbage out. Others, however, can be triggered by a serious issue such as infidelity. Sometimes stress in other areas of your life may negatively affect your marriage. You carry that stress with you and the frustration leaches into your relationships at home. If you want to preserve your marriage, you need to learn how to resolve conflict.

It is your commitment to learning how to resolve conflict that shows your desire to save your marriage. When you have that desire, you can channel that energy into taking constructive steps to identify underlying issues and mend the relationship with your partner. Here are six steps you can take to resolve conflict in your marriage:

1. Keep an open mind

Let go of any preconceived ideas that may prevent you from communicating with your spouse and resolving the conflict. Always accept your partner's ideas, beliefs and opinions even if you don't agree with them. And don't be quick to make assumptions or pass judgment on your spouse's thoughts and feelings.

2. Use humor

Sometimes you and your partner may get stuck in a spiral of retaliation during a conflict. One way to break this pattern is to use humor. This can release pent-up tension and allow you both to focus on mending the relationship rather than engaging in an endless argument. For example, when a conflict starts escalating, both of you can use funny cartoon voices while arguing. If your partner accidentally splashes some water on you at a restaurant, make a joke instead of getting angry. You can jokingly say "He's been spilling water on me for 15 years!" This lightens the mood and allows you to nip a potential conflict in the bud.

3. Show commitment

Be committed to solving the problem — this shows your spouse you are serious about fixing the issue and improving the relationship. One way to show commitment is by maintaining open communication channels where you continually talk to each other about how you feel about things.

4. Attention

Listen carefully whenever your spouse is expressing ideas and opinions about the relationship. And while it can be hard, avoid taking things personally or getting hostile. If they let you speak your truth, you should show them the same courtesy. Practice active listening as described in Chapter Five so you can understand their point of view.

5. Find the root cause

You should identify the conflict's underlying cause so you know what to do to resolve it. Because if you fail to find the real cause, the disagreement will just flare up again and you'll find yourself constantly fighting with your partner.

6. Find a compromise

A marriage only works if both partners feel they have won at the end of the conflict resolution process. You must work to find common ground and create a win-win solution that satisfies both of you. Come up with ground rules that are fair and equal. And agree on a plan for future conflicts. For example, no one will buy expensive items without consulting the other. Once you've agreed on ground rules, you must be willing to forgive each other and take responsibility for implementing the solution.

HELPING CHILDREN HANDLE CONFLICT

We all know that children learn by observing the behavior of the adults. They use their parents as models for learning how to cope with themselves, their peers and the world around them. If you present a model of unhealthy conflict resolution, your children will mimic your style. This can create a problem when they interact with others in the same way. And this is equally a risk if parents fail to present any conflict resolution model at all.

For example, Sally invites her parents and brother to her son's birthday party. During the party, her brother spends his time browsing on his smartphone. Sally tells her brother that he's spending more time on his phone than with his family. He doesn't take this kindly and storms off without a word. As she tries to patch things up with her brother, Sally wonders why he always reacts in anger over small conflicts. After some soul-searching, she realizes that her parents never argued in front of the kids, thus her brother didn't have a model for healthy conflict resolution. Since he didn't see his parents arguing and then resolving their issues, her brother believes that any kind of criticism directed toward him means the other person hates him. He's grown up believing that even a small conflict indicates that the relationship is damaged.

This example shows you the importance of taking active steps to teach kids how to handle conflict. Children experience conflict in their lives just as adults do, but as youngsters, they aren't equipped to effectively deal with the stress that conflict entails. Help your children learn how to handle conflict better. You can show them that conflict is normal and disagreements can be resolved healthily. Keep in mind that your child's ability to resolve conflict will depend on their age, maturity and life experiences. Here are some ideas to help your child deal with conflict:

Teach them conflict doesn't mean the relationship is destroyed

Teach your kids that a disagreement doesn't automatically mean the relationship is damaged. They need to know that it's OK to have opposing views but still get along. If your child tells you their brother has refused to share a toy, explain that it is the action—not the sibling—that's the problem. This helps them understand they shouldn't define their relationship with their brother based on this one event. They will see that one disagreement doesn't mean their brother will always be mean to them in the future.

Show them they are part of the team

Everyone wants to feel like they belong to a group. There's nothing as damaging to a person as feeling ostracized by others, but this is often how you feel when you argue with someone. You can feel as if the other person is rejecting you even when they are simply disagreeing with your point of view. From the previous example, Sally's brother felt she was rejecting him, yet she was only pointing out his behavior. She should have made it clear she didn't have a problem with him—only his actions.

Separating the individual from their behavior is important when teaching children how to manage conflict.

Help them understand that disagreeing doesn't mean they aren't part of the family anymore. If your son argues with his brother over a toy, explain that they still share the same goal despite having different ideas. If the common goal is to play together and have fun, they can take turns playing with the toy instead of competing. Having such conversations with kids may be hard but try to open their minds to look for win-win solutions.

Encourage them to identify and understand their emotions

When you're engaged in a conflict, you experience negative emotions such as anger and fear. These come to the surface, and you then experience sensations such as knots in your stomach, sweaty palms and a pounding heart. Help your children recognize and understand these emotions by verbalizing them when you see your child getting agitated. Gently place your hand on them and ask how they feel. If they can't describe the emotion, you can verbalize it for them. For example, you can tell them, "It looks like you feel angry."

Once you've helped your child identify the emotion, help them explore its cause. For example, "Did you feel angry when your brother refused to share the toy with you?" This will help them stay calm and neutralize the negative emotion. It then becomes easier for them to think of a healthy way to resolve the conflict.

Remember to create a safe environment at home so they can express themselves honestly and openly without fear.

Be a positive role model

Children learn conflict resolution by observing how others resolve their conflicts. If as parents you run to another room to avoid arguing in front of the kids, you are denying your children the opportunity to learn how to resolve conflict. The kids will assume disagreements are bad and should be done in secret. As a child grows into adulthood, they won't know how to handle an open conflict and likely will become avoidant or aggressive. Use conflicts at home as teaching moments so your kids can learn to have honest and healthy conversations about their emotions. You can also act as a role model on how to calm down when angry or anxious. Show them how they can use techniques such as deep breathing, exercise, painting or writing to release negative emotions.

TEACHING CHILDREN COMMUNICATION AND PROBLEM-SOLVING SKILLS

Children need to learn how to communicate effectively during a conflict. Teach them to use "I" statements" to express themselves. For example, "I feel ...

when you say/do ..." And encourage them to not use hurtful words when they disagree with someone. Explain that name-calling hurts the other person's feelings and makes the conflict worse. Teach them the importance of being kind even when the other person is agitated.

You should also teach them how to talk openly and express themselves directly when communicating with others. Use the active listening skills we discussed in Chapter Five to teach them how to listen carefully when others are speaking. Explain how to repeat what the other person says to better understand their argument. Keep in mind that you should model all these behaviors in your conflicts so your kids can learn from you.

You should also teach your kids that problem-solving is another aspect of conflict management. Teach them how to find the cause of the problem as well as solutions. Here are some tips on how to work with your child to build their problem-solving skills:

- Brainstorm to create a long list of solutions.
- Help your child come up with various solutions to the problem.
- Explain the need to be flexible and make compromises when resolving an argument.

- Talk to them about the importance of a win-win solution that meets everyone's needs.
- Help them decide which solution to choose from the list and the actions they should take.
- Help them think of any potential consequences of the chosen solution.
- Provide them with the necessary support as they put the solution into action.

YOUR TWO-MINUTE CONFLICT ACTION PLAN

Before you can teach your child how to manage conflict, you first need to recognize and understand your emotional reactions during a conflict. An easy way to do this is by noticing your body's reactions. When you disagree with your spouse, child, colleague or friend, pay attention to how your body feels. Do you cross your arms? Do you hunch over in fear to protect yourself? Figure out where the tension builds in your body so you can release it. Remind yourself that you shouldn't fight or run from the situation. Instead, use it as an opportunity to connect with the other person on a deeper level to establish a stronger relationship.

RESOLVING WORKPLACE CONFLICTS

Though we've already discussed how you can resolve conflicts within a professional setting (even as a leader), some types of conflict are inevitable in the workplace. These are generational and cultural conflicts. We touched on them in Chapter One but now we're going to go deeper into how to resolve such conflicts.

It's important to study these types of conflict because the workplace is increasingly diverse. People work in teams and are now more interdependent than ever before. In theory, this diversity and interdependence should create greater productivity. But in practice, teams often fail to meet expectations due to unresolved conflict.

Conflicts at the workplace may be commonplace but when they remain unresolved, the organization and individuals suffer. A leader should understand how to navigate the potential conflicts that are likely to arise due to differences in age and cultural background.

Generational conflicts

Your organization has recently acquired a publishing firm that's been in business for 50 years. Most of the editorial staff are 50 and above and have worked there for decades. Your organization decides to inject new blood by hiring college graduates. These younger employees have fresh ideas but are impatient and tend to be short-term thinkers. The older employees focus more on long-term success, discipline and being good negotiators. Due to the firm's changes and new direction, veteran employees begin to retire. As the firm loses older employees with decades of industry knowledge, revenues fall and the firm soon goes under.

This story highlights the clash when different generations work together. With Baby Boomers, Gen X, Millennials and Gen Z all in the workplace, leaders must be adept at juggling a multigenerational workforce with different values, experiences and perspectives. These differences often emerge around specific factors, namely communication, time management, technology usage and organizational structure.

Older generations usually prefer email while younger employees like to text. Older employees are more rigid with their time whereas younger ones are more spontaneous. As a manager of an intergenerational team, consider the tasks involved as well as the collective preferences of the team. For example, the technology should match the task. If the team wants to share daily information, text messages might be used. If the team wants to brainstorm, video chats may work better. This way, the different generations are catered to, and fewer conflicts arise.

But how do you handle generational conflicts when they do arise? Here are five steps to take:

1. **Acknowledge** – Talk to your team about generational differences that exist between team members. Acknowledging such differences makes it easier to solve any problems that may result from generational gaps.
2. **Appreciate** – Encourage your team to focus on "why" the team is working together rather than "what" they are working on. The "why" represents the common goals and unites people.
3. **Flex** – Encourage your employees to be flexible and adopt a variety of approaches that cater to the preferences of different generations.
4. **Leverage** – Take advantage of the strengths of the different generations. Let those who are more experienced using specific technologies mentor those who aren't.
5. **Resolve** – When being flexible isn't working, identify the option that yields the best results.

Dismantling stereotypes and creating unity

Generational differences at the workplace sometimes lead to stereotyping and discrimination on a subtle level. As a manager, you must be aware of your values and beliefs because they may cause you to be biased against a specific group of employees in your team. For example, you may unintentionally be skewing work distribution based on age rather than merit. You may be assuming younger employees are better with technology so you quit giving technological assignments to older employees.

Instead of discriminating against a generation, identify each person's unique value. Gauge an employee's competence based on their strengths and weaknesses. And recognize and create synergy between employees with different perspectives and experiences. Use team-building exercises and sporting activities to promote collaboration and trust. The more the different generations share their life experiences, the more they'll value each other.

And the more they value each other's contribution to the team, the more they'll unite around a common purpose. Productivity and customer service will improve as team members become better aligned with each other. Each member may have their strengths and preferences but the most important thing is to create a sense of unity to accomplish common goals.

Cultural conflicts

Your cultural background has a great influence on how you live and work. And it also affects how you approach conflict. When you work with individuals from diverse cultures, look for culturally distinct ways to make decisions, communicate and solve problems. These pathways will help the team resolve conflicts when they arise.

Cultural conflicts are not necessarily based on differences in ethnicity, tribe, clan or nationality. Sometimes a team may have members who simply have different beliefs and behaviors despite having seemingly identical backgrounds. So, it's important not to ignore the real differences that exist between people. At the same time, you should avoid generalizing people based on the culture they come from. There are always some individuals who don't conform to their dominant cultural narrative.

This is especially true in western societies where individual tendencies are highly valued. Western culture is predominantly individualistic and values such as creativity, autonomy and initiative are highly prized. In other parts of the world, a collective culture dominates where the interests of the group trump those of the individual.

This distinction between individual and collective cultures is important because both groups handle conflict differently. Individualists perceive conflict as normal and handle it in the open. Collectivists see conflict as a social failure, so they pretend to get along just to avoid social embarrassment.

How does this play out in a team experiencing conflict? In most cases, collective team members prefer to resolve conflict internally instead of getting outside help. On the other hand, the individualists prefer to bring in someone who has no relationship with the team. This could be an external mediator or an HR representative. When they do involve an external mediator, collectivists expect the mediator to have the final say on the dispute. This is contrary to the individual culture where the mediator only plays an evaluative or facilitative role.

Culture also affects the way people communicate with one another. In some cultures, expressing emotions through touching and extended eye contact is normal. And other cultures may prefer a communication style that is more stoic, unemotional and eye contact is avoided. This is not to say that one culture is better than the other. The problem is that sometimes a person from one culture will judge their colleague based on their own communication style. For example, a colleague who disagrees forcefully by raising their voice may be perceived as arrogant by someone whose culture promotes restraint. A colleague from a culture that prefers directness may judge teammates harshly for beating around the bush as they perceive this to be a waste of time.

These kinds of judgments will also influence the way individuals negotiate to resolve a conflict. In western cultures, people tend to negotiate based on their underlying interests rather than haggling over positions. Some cultures tend to focus on time and rules when negotiating a conflict. Individuals from such cultures want the negotiation process to have a definitive start and end rather than be a continual process. They may also prefer to have clear rules and order during the meeting rather than focus on the emotional aspects of the relationship.

Lessons to learn

Having a multicultural team at work poses several challenges when it comes to conflict management and resolution. There are some lessons you can learn to effectively handle cultural conflicts. Here are seven simple strategies to follow:

- **Know your culture** – Explore your values and biases so you can be more open to diverse opinions. When you're aware of your social-political culture, it's easier to compare and contrast without feeling threatened by other cultures.
- **Learn other cultures** – Talk to your team members about their cultures and how they handle conflict. Watch movies and read books to better understand other cultures.
- **Clarify, don't assume** – If a colleague avoids eye contact while you are speaking to them, don't assume they are being hostile. Approach them and ask for clarification on that particular behavior. Tell them how their behavior affected you. For example, "I noticed you weren't making eye contact during our discussion. Maybe you were bored but I felt ignored when you did that. What was going on?"
- **Ask questions** – When you join an existing team, you're going to face an existing team culture. And while you want to respect the culture, you should also ask questions to clarify why things are done a particular way.
- **Listen** – Practice active listening to learn the norms of other cultures. Listening enables team

members to compromise when there is a clash of cultural norms.
- **Follow the platinum rule** – Treat your colleagues as they want to be treated rather than the way you want to be treated. Empathize with them to gain a better perspective of their side of the conflict.
- **Conflict is multicultural** – Conflicts stem from miscommunication and communication is always either intracultural or intercultural. Even within a culture, you'll find people with independent beliefs and values. Therefore, all conflicts are multicultural, and you should be prepared to use cross-cultural communication at all times.

CHAPTER TAKEAWAYS

As a leader, when a conflict arises between your employees, you can either intervene or let them work it out. Don't interfere too much unless you have to. But there are things you can do to ensure a conflict-free workplace. These are some simple steps you can take as a leader:

- Encourage your employees to resolve any basic conflict themselves instead of running to you for a resolution. This will gradually equip them to co-exist peacefully and also train them to deal with bigger conflicts in the future.

- Some employees won't be confident in their ability to resolve workplace conflict and may want to involve you all the time. Coach them on how to resolve conflicts. Use the four-stage approach described in Chapters Five to Nine to help them understand the conflict resolution process. You can role-play with them to familiarize them with conflict situations and the appropriate responses.

- Maintain open communication channels with your employees so they can give you feedback on your level of involvement in office conflicts. Talk to your employees and encourage them to be open with what they think or feel. If they speak their mind, pay attention and take it seriously. The information they give will help you know if you're too involved, too aloof or if your involvement is appropriate.

- There will be some conflicts your employees won't be able to handle. If such a situation arises, you'll have to intervene. Talk to those involved to identify and clarify the problem. Ensure you lay out ground rules for engagement and encourage both sides to actively listen to each other. Coach them on the stages of negotiation and planning as described in Chapter 10. This will help them find areas of agreement and facilitate brainstorming. And encourage them to identify viable solutions as well as alternative approaches to resolve the conflict. Ask them to create a resolution plan based on the information they have gathered. If they are unable to do so, you can step in and help them identify the best course of action. Encourage them to collaborate to implement this plan and set up a schedule of meetings to track progress. Let them know that if they feel the plan is not working, they are free to change it up.

In the next and final chapter, you'll learn how to create your conflict resolution plan.

12

MAKING YOUR OWN CONFLICT RESOLUTION PLAN

We've already established that conflict is a normal and healthy aspect of relationships. People will always find something to disagree on at some point in time. And so it's essential to learn how to deal with conflicts in a way that doesn't damage the relationship. If you learn how to handle conflicts positively, you will grow as an individual and the relationship will get stronger. This is how you should perceive any conflict you experience in your personal and professional life.

In previous chapters, we talked about what conflict is and how to manage it in your personal as well as professional relationships. This chapter is a summary of the most important points and the skills you need to resolve conflicts. Use this information to create your plans to manage difficult situations whenever you find yourself in a conflict.

As you create your conflict resolution plan, take into account two factors. The first is your emotional response to the conflict and the second is the impact the conflict has on the relationship. Keeping these in mind can help you stay focused so that you resolve the disagreement without harming your relationship with that individual. Your plan should be based on a clear understanding of the fundamentals of conflict resolution and the tools you use to get to the root cause of the conflict.

UNDERSTAND THE FUNDAMENTALS

Successful conflict resolution is only possible if you understand the fundamentals of the resolution process. It's easy to blow up and verbally attack the other person when you're angry but acting this way only makes the situation worse. There are four specific skills you should focus on when making your plan. These are:

- **Stress management** – Practice staying calm during heated exchanges. This helps to accurately read and interpret the other person's signals.
- **Emotional control** – Don't take things

personally. Controlling your emotions helps you express yourself more clearly.
- **Paying attention to what's being said** – Actively listen to the other person and watch their body language.
- **Being respectful** – Respect the other person's ideas and opinions.

These skills are a lifeline for every leader who wants to stay on top of their conflict resolution game. If you want to resolve your conflicts respectfully and positively, you must keep these abilities sharpened.

USE EMPATHY WISELY

Empathy is a key tool you'll need when dealing with conflicts with people who are close to your heart. For example, if you're arguing with a family member or friend, you cannot risk burning the relationship to the ground. You need to be empathetic so that the person you care about feels heard and understood. This also applies to conflicts in official situations. When a colleague or employee tells you they feel unheard, cheated or lost, you should empathize and help them calm down.

But empathy is not required in every situation. Some conflicts only need a logical process to resolve the issue.

Showing empathy in such situations may make the problem more complicated. For example, you and a team member want to adopt different methods to complete a task and a conflict erupts. In this case, empathy doesn't help resolve the disagreement. When you're involved in this kind of conflict, you should evaluate your decisions based on the following criteria:

- Does ceding ground to the other party result in a quick resolution of the conflict and progression of the task? If so, accommodate their idea without complicating things.
- Does one method have a greater benefit than the other in terms of conserving resources? If so, choose that method.

Based on the example above, you and your colleague should always discuss the conflict after the task has been completed. This will help you both come to an agreement based on an understanding of the shared goals of the team.

PICK YOUR BATTLES

You need to know which battles to fight and which ones to let go. Not all conflicts can be resolved the same way, and some don't require a win-win solution. For example, if you're having a conflict with a friend or family member, evaluate your options and act according to the value of that relationship. You are invested in that relationship for the long haul, maybe even a lifetime. Step back and think about how escalating the conflict may impact the relationship. If you truly value the relationship, it shouldn't be too difficult to apologize and fix the mistakes you made. Compromise isn't a weakness. It shows the other person that you truly care.

The way you handle a conflict in an organizational setting may be different. If you're in a conflict with a colleague and you feel the situation is beyond you, ask your superior to intervene. If you're in a leadership position and a minor conflict arises between your team members, encourage them to resolve the issue on their own. Certain small arguments don't require your input at all. Just remind them to focus on the shared goals of the team and organization. As a leader, you need to promote cooperation and collaboration to create a positive work environment for your team to achieve its goals.

CONFLICT IS ABOUT PERSPECTIVE

The way you handle conflict is determined by your perspective. Most people engage in conflict to win and have their way. However, the end goal of negotiation isn't always about getting what you want. As described in Chapter Three, a collaborative approach is the best way to resolve disagreements. It allows people to come together to find a way of mitigating problems. Though the process may be a long one, working together allows you to gain insight into the other person's thoughts and actions. It also enables you both to see how to complete each other's weaknesses to reach a better understanding.

You should also understand that conflicts aren't always bad. They have many positive aspects such as promoting better companionship, strengthening bonds and helping people understand how they fit into the bigger picture of life. From now on, start to see conflict differently. Think of it as a character arc in a movie or novel, letting you evolve into a better version of yourself. Don't shy away from conflicts but also don't actively seek them. Most importantly, mitigate any issues when you see them arise so they don't explode into full-blown conflict. If a conflict does occur, don't wait too long to resolve it. The longer you wait, the worse it gets.

CONCLUSION

There's one main point I really want you to take away from this book—conflicts are part and parcel of our lives and avoiding them only makes matters worse. In this book, we have talked about some of the reasons why people avoid conflict. The most common is fear of hurting others and ending up with a painful outcome once a conflict ends. These fears are the result of your childhood, especially how your parents, teachers and friends treated you. It is due to this childhood trauma and the painful emotions still haunting you that your brain instinctively prefers to avoid conflicts.

But you shouldn't avoid conflict just because of childhood programming. Conflicts can be beneficial if handled correctly. It allows both parties to come to a mutual understanding of how each side works and the goals they share. Conflict can help you see a different side of life, so you expand your thinking and become more open to others' opinions. Embracing the positive aspects of conflict lets you learn how to manage it effectively.

There are five types of conflict management strategies that you can use. But you'll probably ou find two of them are the most effective once you start accepting conflicts rather than avoiding them. They are accommodation and collaboration. In accommodation, you compromise some of your gains for the benefit of the other party. In collaboration, you actively work with the other party to find a win-win solution that favors both sides.

As you adopt these two conflict management strategies, you will learn important skills such as:

- **Staying calm** – Keep a level head and manage your emotions. You can engage in breathing techniques or even go for a walk to calm your emotions. You should also take time to think before responding to the other person's words.
- **Active listening** – Pay attention to the other person's words and body language without passing any form of judgment.
- **Empathy** – Tap into your emotions to

understand the perspectives of others. Put yourself in the shoes of the other person to understand why they think the way they do. Empathy also helps you understand why they escalated the issue into a conflict.
- **Focus** – Once you and the other party understand each other, focus on shared goals and how you can work together to resolve the issue.
- **Negotiation** – Brainstorm with the other party to collect ideas and solutions on how to resolve the conflict without incurring heavy losses on either side.

At the end of the day, no matter how bad the conflict gets, try to forgive, and forget. People can say nasty things in the heat of the moment and these personal comments can feel like sharp jabs. But just because the other person has failed to maintain their composure doesn't mean you should lose control. Even after the conflict is resolved, you still have to work with that colleague or still live with your spouse. So harboring grudges, negative opinions and baseless judgments won't help you. The best thing to do if you can is to let go of these feelings and forgive the other person.

KEY TAKEAWAYS

Here are the four quick hacks or phases in resolving conflicts:

1. **In Phase I**, you listen to what the other person has to say without interrupting them, then create ground rules that facilitate open communication. Make sure each party is given a fair hearing and is well understood. Don't let your emotions get the better of you. Acknowledge what they have to say and diffuse any highly charged emotions quickly to avoid losing control of the situation.
2. **In Phase II**, use empathy and validation to understand the needs and wants of the other party. Make sure that before you move forward, both parties have established a mutual understanding of the situation and are ready to collaborate to achieve a common goal.
3. **In Phase III**, identify the common goal and determine how both parties can reach it. During the negotiation, maintain goodwill and a positive attitude. If you feel a conflict threatens your relationship, try to resolve this first and see how you can save this bond. If you feel there's little you can do to resolve the issue,

involve a mediator. If things get worse, accept the outcome and walk away. Make sure to forgive and forget.

4. **In Phase IV**, dive into the root cause of the conflict and come up with an action plan that eliminates the problem and brings solutions. Use brainstorming to help both parties reach a mutually agreeable and satisfactory goal. Try to minimize the damage as much as you can. A few compromises are acceptable as long as both parties see eye to eye. Once your plan is ready, put it into motion and regularly check in with all parties to see if it needs any adjustments to improve the end goal.

My goal with this book is to provide you with a clear path to handle conflicts and manage various situations. Now you are equipped to break out of your fear so you can take life back into your hands. Even if you hate conflicts, the steps laid out here will help you avoid overthinking whenever you're in a conflict situation. And hopefully, you will always arrive at an acceptable solution.

Has this book helped you resolve conflicts in your life? Do you feel you're in a better place now and more evolved than you were before?

If so, share your story of overcoming conflicts with us. Head over to Amazon and leave a review of this book so we can learn about your journey of conflict management. We'd love to hear from you!

DISCUSSION SECTION

Here are some key points worth mentioning:

1. As a leader, you should embrace conflict and deal with it constructively. An inability to handle conflict in an organization may lead to consequences such as lost time, low productivity, grievances and reports to employee tribunals. It also destroys creativity and expertise. Handling conflict constructively leads to the strengthening of team harmony, creation of growth opportunities and innovation of new products and services.

2. To embrace conflict, you must:

- Reframe your perspective on what conflict means. See its benefits instead of focusing only on its negative aspects.
- Interrogate your organization's culture to see if it's open to constructive criticism. Are people victimized for expressing their opinions? Create a culture where employees are allowed

to take risks and make mistakes. This form of continuous improvement and growth must be led by top management.
- If the organization's culture stifles open dialogue, create a safe space where people can openly challenge the status quo. Allow your team to engage in sessions where they critique old practices and come up with new ones. If someone makes a mistake, tell your team to focus on solutions rather than attacking the person who messed up..

3. Find which conflict management style you naturally rely on when dealing with conflicts. Are you avoiding, compromising, competing, accommodating, or collaborating? Take an assessment test such as the one provided at the end of Chapter Three to evaluate yourself. Once you identify your dominant style, decide if you should change it. Remember that the ideal conflict styles are accommodating and collaborating. Aim to learn these and then adopt them as your conflict style, too. Conflict is usually triggered by perceptions that don't accurately reflect the other person's intentions. So ask questions at various stages of the conflict resolution process. Questions create empathy and trust. They also help you understand the other person's perceptions so you can agree on

possible solutions. Some questions you can ask include:

- *How did that make you feel?*
- *What emotions am I feeling due to this conflict?*
- *What can we do to fix this relationship?*
- *What can I do to show you that I'm worthy of your trust?*
- *How did you perceive my words/behavior?*
- *How is this conflict helping me?*
- *What am I not willing to accept?*

Again, wherever people come together, there is the possibility of conflict. This book has given you insights on how to resolve differences anytime, anywhere, and with anyone. Included tools that allow you to understand your style and those of others around you and learn about various tools available so you can customize the ideal solution to any dispute. To receive the Conflict Management Quiz, go to: https://marlenegonzalez.com/conflicted or scan the QR code below!

CONCLUSION | 263

PRAISE FOR MARLENE GONZALEZ

Dear Reader,

I hope you like it!

As a self-publishing author, I rely on readers like you to help promote my work and serve humanity better by doing my best to write, share, coach and train the next generation of leaders like you.

Please consider posting an online review on Amazon, a short review, audio, or a picture highlighting the page you enjoyed the most because reviews are essential to the success of any book. They help potential buyers make confident decisions when choosing and buying books. Just scan the QR code below!

Thank you for taking this journey with me,

Your coach, Marlene Gonzalez.

ABOUT THE AUTHOR

Marlene Gonzalez is the founder and the president of Life coaching group LLC. focusing on Leadership development and executive coaching. She passionately pursues one vision- "To advance, develop and promote minority leaders." She is a renowned executive coach and facilitator. She is the author of the coaching series Leadership Wizard; "Number 1 New Release book in the Education and Leadership category". Her book series specializes in transformational leadership topics such as:

Leadership Wizard. The Nine Dimensions. Unlock the Leader in You. The Discipline of Coaching Yourself to Fearlessly Lead, Influence, Inspire and Empower Others.

Assertive Wizard. How To Boost Confidence, Get Your Message Across, And Speak with Impact.

Change Wizard. Master The Art of Leading Change and Working Together for a Common Purpose.

Confident Wizard. Turn Self Doubt into Confidence: The Ultimate Guide to Lead With Authenticity, Purpose, and Resilience.

Once you master these and many other topics she covers, you can transform your life and become a more successful leader. In addition, you will find that her books have a straight-to-the-point approach and easy to implement actions. She is passionate about sharing her insights and resources on transformational leadership through a combination of Insights Discovery, the psychology of C. G. Jung, her corporate career experience, and her professional coaching expertise.

González held many executive corporate positions in the US, Europe, and Latin America. She is the former Senior Director of Global Training, Learning, and Development for McDonald's Corporation. Marlene holds a BS, an Executive MBA/PAG, and a graduate diploma on managerial Issues in the global enterprise from Thunderbird University. www. marlenegonzalez.com

ALSO BY MARLENE GONZALEZ

AVAILABLE ON AUDIBLE

THE SELF COACHING GUIDE TO MASTER THE ART OF LEADERSHIP AND CHANGE LIKE A PRO

Two in One Bundle

Leadership comes from within, but you can't find it until you know where to look. Here's what you need to know...The power is within you to become a true wizard!

Sign up Now

to get free resources and more!

REFERENCES

Alhattab, F. (Sept. 30, 2020). Why You Should Embrace Conflict in the Workplace. *Unicorn Labs.* Retrieved from https://www.unicornlabs.ca/blog/why-you-should-embrace-conflict-in-the-workplace

Amaresan, S. (June 9, 2021). 27 conflict resolution skills to use with your team and your customers. *Hubspot.* Retrieved from https://blog.hubspot.com/service/conflict-resolution-skills

American Sentinel College of Nursing & Health Sciences. (Sept. 29, 2015). Conflict in the workplace: Bridging the generation gap. Retrieved from https://www.americansentinel.edu/blog/2015/09/29/conflict-in-the-workplace-bridging-the-generation-gap/

Barth, F.D. (Oct. 1, 2017). Are you conflict avoidant or conflict seeking? *Psychology Today*. Retrieved from https://www.psychologytoday.com/us/blog/the-couch/201710/are-you-conflict-avoidant-or-conflict-seeking

Canfield, C. (Dec. 1, 2016). The beauty of conflict. *YouTube*. Retrieved from https://www.youtube.com/watch?v=55n9pH_A0O8

Chand, S. Conflict management: Characteristics, types, stages, causes, and other details. https://www.yourarticlelibrary.com/business/conflict-management-characteristics-types-stages-causes-and-other-details/5431

Conflicts Dynamics Profile. The trouble with avoiding conflict. Retrieved from https://www.conflictdynamics.org/the-trouble-with-avoiding-conflict-2/

DeMarco, J. (Oct. 3, 2018). Why am I so afraid of conflict? A therapist weighs in. *The Every Girl*. Retrieved from https://theeverygirl.com/why-am-i-so-afraid-of-conflict/

Eather, R. What clouds your judgment in times of stress? – A mindful way to move through our stress responses. *Brisbane Natural Health*. Retrieved from https://brisbanenaturalhealth.com/what-clouds-your-judgment-in-times-of-stress-a-mindful-way-to-move-through-our-stress-responses/

Fabrega, M. 8 ways to stop taking things personally. https://daringtolivefully.com/stop-taking-things-personally

Feigenbaum, E. Differences and conflict in diversity. *Chron.* Retrieved from https://smallbusiness.chron.com/differences-conflict-diversity-3045.html

Ford, J. (October 2001). Cross-cultural conflict resolution in teams. Retrieved from https://www.mediate.com/articles/ford5.cfm

Funsten, R. (Oct. 19, 2016). How understanding conflict can help improve our lives. *YouTube.* Retrieved from https://www.youtube.com/watch?v=fdDQSHyyUic

Frey, W.H. (Jan. 26, 2018). Old vs. young: The cultural generation gap. *PEW.* Retrieved from https://www.pewtrusts.org/en/trend/archive/winter-2018/old-versus-young-the-cultural-generation-gap

Friedman, R. (Jan. 12, 2016). Defusing an emotionally charged conversation with a colleague. *Harvard Business Review.* Retrieved from https://hbr.org/2016/01/defusing-an-emotionally-charged-conversation-with-a-colleague

Frye, T. Teaching Your Kids How to Resolve Conflict Without Fighting. *A Fine Parent.* Retrieved on Sept. 21,

2021. https://afineparent.com/be-positive/how-to-resolve-conflict.html

Gallo, A. (June 16, 2014.) Choose the right words in an argument. Harvard Business Review. Retrieved from https://hbr.org/2014/06/choose-the-right-words-in-an-argument

Hello Seven. (March 31, 2019). How to have a successful confrontation (even if you hate conflict). Retrieved from https://helloseven.co/how-to-have-a-successful-confrontation-even-if-you-hate-conflic

Hirsch, A. (Feb. 5, 2020). How to manage intergenerational conflict in the workplace. Retrieved from https://www.shrm.org/resourcesandtools/hr-topics/employee-relations/pages/how-to-manage-intergenerational-conflict-in-the-workplace.aspx

Ilgaz, Z. (May 15, 2014). Conflict resolution: When should leaders step in? Forbes. Retrieved from https://www.forbes.com/sites/85broads/2014/05/15/conflict-resolution-when-should-leaders-step-in/?sh=1ba62bc43357

Jacobson, S. (March 22, 2017). The benefits of conflict resolution. Conover. Retrieved from https://www.conovercompany.com/the-benefits-of-conflict-resolution/

Janse, B. (2020). Drill Down Technique. *ToolsHero.* https://www.toolshero.com/problem-solving/drill-down-technique/

Johnston, S. (2017). Great Leaders Embrace Conflict. *HealthManagement, Vol 17 – Issue 3.* https://healthmanagement.org/c/healthmanagement/issuearticle/great-leaders-embrace-conflict

Juneja, P. Understanding conflict: Meaning and phases of conflict. *Management Study Guide.* Retrieved from https://www.managementstudyguide.com/understanding-conflict.htm.

Juneja, P. Conflict at the workplace: Why conflict should be avoided? *Management Study Guide.* Retrieved from https://www.managementstudyguide.com/conflict-at-workplace.htm

Kaur, G. (Aug. 24, 2016). Cultural conflicts in organizations. *Slideshare.* Retrieved from https://www.slideshare.net/GurpreetTamber3/cultural-conflicts-in-organisations

Kids Helpline. (July 13, 2018). Helping kids handle conflict. https://kidshelpline.com.au/parents/issues/helping-kids-handle-conflict

Madsen, T.B. (March 8, 2017). Active Listening: The Most Undervalued Skill in Conflict Situations. *HuffPost.*

https://www.huffpost.com/entry/active-listening-the-most-undervalued-skill-in-conflict_b_58be73d7e4b0aeb52475fed7

Marcus and Ashley. Resolving Conflict In Marriage: How To Resolve Conflicts With Your Spouse Peacefully. *Our Peaceful Family.* https://ourpeacefulfamily.com/resolving-conflict-in-marriage/

Markman, H., Stanley, S., & Blumberg, S.L. (1994). Fighting for your marriage. *San Francisco: Josey-Bass Publishers.* Retrieved from https://www3.nd.edu/~pmtrc/Handouts/Ground_Rules_3.pdf

McLeod, L.E. (Sept. 5, 2011). Why avoiding conflict keeps you trapped in it forever. *HuffPost.* Retrieved from https://www.huffpost.com/entry/why-avoiding-conflict-kee_b_891460

MindTools. Appreciation (Situational): Understanding the Full Implications of a Fact. Retrieved from https://www.mindtools.com/pages/article/newTMC_01.htm

MindTools. Empathy at work: Developing skills to understand other people. Retrieved from https://www.mindtools.com/pages/article/EmpathyatWork.htm

MindTools. 5 Whys: Getting to the root of a problem quickly. Retrieved from https://www.mindtools.com/pages/article/newTMC_5W.htm

Mockler, S. Not all conflicts are created equal: The 3 types of conflict. *Vantage*. Retrieved from https://www.vantageleadership.com/our-blog/not-all-conflicts-are-equal-3-types-of-conflict/

Novak, M.C. (May 14, 2019). 5 most effective conflict management styles (+when to use each one). *Learn*. Retrieved from https://learn.g2.com/conflict-management-styles

Oglethorpe, A. (Feb. 15, 2019). The secrets to keeping your cool during conflict. *MM Lafleur*. Retrieved from https://mmlafleur.com/mdash/how-to-stay-calm-during-conflict-at-work.

Pearson, C.M. (March 13, 2017). The smart way to respond to negative emotions at work. *MIT Sloan Management Review*. Retrieved from https://sloanreview.mit.edu/article/the-smart-way-to-respond-to-negative-emotions-at-work/

Pursey, K. (Aug. 8, 2017). How to remain calm during any argument or conflict situation, backed by science. *Learning mind*. https://www.learning-mind.com/how-to-remain-calm/

Rensburg, M. (March 18, 2017). A child's subconscious mind: How parents can hurt or help their kids. *Medianet*.
https://www.medianet.com.au/releases/128343/

Robbins, T. How to use "I-statements"; changing your words will change your relationship. *The Tony Robbins Blog.* Retrieved from https://www.tonyrobbins.com/love-relationships/words-matter-you-vs-i/. Accessed on Sept. 21, 2021.

Robinson, L., Segal, J. & Smith, M. (October 2020). Conflict resolution skills. *HelpGuide.* Retrieved from https://www.helpguide.org/articles/relationships-communication/conflict-resolution-skills.htm

Robinson, L., Segal, J. & Smith, M. (October 2020). Nonverbal communication and body language. *HelpGuide.* Retrieved from https://www.helpguide.org/articles/relationships-communication/nonverbal-communication.htm

Root Cause Analysis: Tracing a Problem to Its Origins. https://www.mindtools.com/pages/article/newTMC_80.htm

Sharma, R. (Sept. 13, 2017). Why do we avoid taking risks? *Medium.* Retrieved from https://medium.com/romasharma/why-do-we-avoid-taking-risks-1f3e5799004b

Shonk, K. (Oct. 1, 2020). 3 types of conflict and how to address them: Different types of conflict—including task conflict, relationship conflict, and value conflict—can benefit from different approaches to conflict resolution. Harvard Law School. Retrieved from https://www.pon.harvard.edu/daily/conflict-resolution/types-conflict/

SkillsYouNeed. What is Negotiation? Retrieved from https://www.skillsyouneed.com/ips/negotiation.html

Smalley, G. (September 2015.) Validation is the third step to conflict resolution in L.U.V.E. Retrieved from https://www.focusonthefamily.com/marriage/validation-is-the-third-step-to-conflict-resolution-in-l-u-v-e/

Talent Tools. (June 7, 2018). The benefits of effective conflict management = benefits of conflict competence. Retrieved from https://www.talenttools.com.au/articles/the-benefits-of-effective-conflict-management---benefits-of-conflict-competence.html

Terry, J. The high cost of unresolved conflict. *Tercon-Partners.* https://terconpartners.com/the-high-cost-of-unresolved-conflict/

The Color Works. Insights discovery color energies: A beginner's guide. Retrieved from https://www.thecolourworks.com/insights-discovery-colour-types-guide/

The Conflict Expert. (Aug. 27, 2019). Is now a good time to talk? How to tell when a conflict is ripe for resolution. Retrieved from https://the-conflictexpert.com/2019/08/27/is-now-a-good-time-to-talk-how-to-tell-when-a-conflict-is-ripe-for-resolution/

The Conflict Expert. (April 8, 2019). How empathy can resolve and prevent conflict. Retrieved from https://the-conflictexpert.com/2019/04/08/how-empathy-can-resolve-and-prevent-conflict/

The Conflict Expert. (June 20, 2019). 42 questions to help resolve conflict. https://the-conflictexpert.com/2019/06/20/42-questions-to-help-resolve-conflict/

Valamis. (May 14, 2020). Conflict management styles. Retrieved from https://www.valamis.com/hub/conflict-management-styles

Wearebowline. (Oct. 31, 2017). 8 personality types: a deeper dive into insights discovery. Retrieved from https://www.wearebowline.com/blog/8-personality-types-a-deeper-dive-into-insights-discovery/

West, H. (Sept. 13, 2017). Why do people avoid conflict? Retrieved from http://www.harperwest.co/why-do-people-avoid-conflict/

www.ingramcontent.com/pod-product-compliance
Lightning Source LLC
Chambersburg PA
CBHW030112240426
43673CB00002B/51